God

A Scientific Update

The Bible dates back a couple of thousand years. It describes reality—that is, the world, mankind, and God—based on the wisdom of the time. Current knowledge offers a considerably improved foundation for understanding issues of relevance to religion; thus, it is time for an update.

I believe the time is also ripe for resolving the conflict between science and religion, as religion has a lot to offer society. Science can tell us how we ought to deal with the world; religion can help us get there. As Einstein once said, "Science without religion is lame, religion without science is blind."

—BJØRN GRINDE

GOD
A SCIENTIFIC UPDATE

BJØRN GRINDE

The Darwin Press, Inc.
Princeton, New Jersey

Publisher's Cataloging-In-Publication Data
(Prepared by The Donohue Group, Inc.)

Grinde, Bjørn, 1952-
  God : a scientific update / Bjørn Grinde.

  p. : ill. ; cm.

  Includes bibliographical references and index.
  ISBN: 978-0-87850-184-7

  1. Religion and science. 2. Modernist-fundamentalist controversy. 3. Civilization, Modern. 4. Religions--Relations. 5. God. 6. Spirituality.
  I. Title.

BL240.3 .G75 2010
215

All photos in this publication were taken by the author.

Published by: The Darwin Press, Inc., Princeton, NJ 08543-2202 USA

Printed in the United States of America

Contents

Text Figures

Preface

God has been caught in the crossfire, and has become a focal element in many of the conflicts tormenting the world today. It is tempting to appeal to spirituality in times of tension—tempting because religion has the power to bring people together, and because it is easy to define enemies based on differences in belief. Thus, wars are made in the name of God, and faith is used to suppress opponents. In either case religion is blamed.

God is also under fire from a different angle; the discord between science and faith causes almost as much controversy as recruiting God for duty in time of war. The conflict between science and religion, in combination with the association between faith and aggression, has produced considerable aversion toward any form of spirituality. The critique is relevant and yet somewhat unfair. True, most religions have been involved in some sordid affairs, but that is not the complete picture. Mass media are partly responsible. Drawn toward conflicts, journalists tend to create a biased depiction; their focus is on the negative aspects of religion such as war, terrorism, and repression. The positive qualities are rarely discussed. A vast number of people have found considerable comfort and joy in faith, and most religions are primarily aimed at helping strangers, rather than killing them. Thus, religions not only promote hostility, but they are also deeply involved in alleviating calamities by appealing to compassion and tolerance. In order to obtain an unbiased view, it is essential to consider carefully what impact religion really has on society.

The question is: What carries most weight? What if all that has happened in the name of God should be added to a balance scale—the good on one side, and the bad on the other—without considering whether it is appropriate to put the blame, or praise, on God. In a way, this would be "A Day of Judgment for the Divine." My discussion presumes that the side of the balance scale with the good will hit the ground.

Then again, history is not giving us the answer we ought to seek; it is the future we should care about—not the past. It is conceivable that a hundred years from now people will not even consider bringing out the scale. Depending on how we are able to reap the potential that is present in human spirituality, the contribution of future creeds to improving society may be vastly superior to what we have seen in the past.

It is important to keep in mind that, biologically speaking, humans have not changed appreciably over the last 100,000 years, and are unlikely to do so in the next thousands of years. Our innate tendencies towards spirituality will remain—as will our predispositions for both violence and compassion. We need to make the most of human nature as it is. Taking advantage of human spirituality may prove a highly rational stance.

When it comes to improving the condition of humankind, science and religion both have crucial contributions to offer. If we are to benefit from mankind's spiritual propensity, we need a platform that deals with the following three issues: One, how to reconcile science with religion; two, how to create tolerance among different religious doctrines; and three, how to strengthen the positive aspects of human spirituality. I believe a first step towards creating such a platform is to update the religious perspectives with regard to our present knowledge. That is the main topic of this book.

The concept of God has many denotations. In the Western world most people associate God with the Christian God, but human spirituality is far more diverse. Mankind has generated numerous belief systems, and those with us today are continuously changing. Skepticism toward certain aspects of any particular creed should, therefore, not be considered grounds for rejecting religiousness altogether. It is possible to find ways of worship that avoid the conflicts mentioned above.

No creed remains untouched by the shifts of society. On the other hand, arbitrary changes, whether in religious doctrine or other aspects of human culture, are not necessarily improvements. Thus, the important question is how to use human ingenuity to improve, or bring out the best in, our systems of faith.

For me, the concept of God includes all types of spiritual worship. The Divine Force I describe is meant to be a common denominator for the various creeds. The concept can be given a minimum of content by associating it with the creation of the Universe. Whether or not God exists is then a semantic question.

Not so many years ago scientists assumed that the Universe had always been there; today we are fairly certain it had a beginning.

The term "God" can be used as a name for the foundation or origin of our Universe or as a name for what constitutes the Universe. I hope those who have an aversion toward the word "God" will consider the use of the word herein with an open mind.

The first two chapters add substance to this concept of God. The following two chapters deal with two topics that are close to the core of most denominations: The third chapter details the current model for what the Universe is and how it came into existence, i.e., the Story of Creation, while the fourth chapter adds advice about how one ought to pursue life, including the question of a moral code. The final chapter looks to the future.

———

The Bible based its Genesis and its moral commandments on the knowledge available at the time. The purpose was to help people understand and relate to the world they lived in, including how to interact with fellow human beings. Over the course of the past two thousand years, there has been an enormous expansion of knowledge. Unfortunately, it has proven difficult for Christianity, or for that matter other religions, to adapt to these advances. The abyss separating the secular and spiritual aspects of society has widened to such an extent that it seems nearly impossible to find a way across.

I believe, however, that it *is* possible to close this abyss or, at least, to construct a bridge over it—without compromising either faith or science. With this as my goal, I shall describe our present scientific understanding of the Universe and life on Earth, but at the same time suggest a spiritual way of sensing the world. My intention is to create a basis for those denominations that wish to adapt to present realities. Science is difficult to avoid. Yet, as will be explained, this does not necessarily mean the various faiths need to reject their own visions and principles.

Human spirituality has a considerable potential for improving society. Although science *provides* us with knowledge, religion is important when it comes to *utilizing* present wisdom. Commandments from God have certain advantages, when compared to laws or professional recommendations, in that there is a tendency for people to prefer spiritual advice.

———

This book contains *footnotes* with comments and references for further reading. Although much of the relevant information can be found on the Internet, I tend to avoid Internet addresses—because they are volatile and because relevant pages can generally be found using keywords from the text. Also included are text figures and appendixes for the purpose of providing supplementary information pertaining to particular subjects. The book is illustrated with photographs taken by the author and meant to reflect religious sentiments. An *index* concludes the book.

Chapel in an Isanzu village, Tanzania.

Acknowledgments

The author would like to thank the following people for valuable comments: David Elboth, Thomas Hylland Eriksen, Dagfinn Føllesdal, Sigrid Gjellan, Steinar Grinde, Dag Olav Hessen, Helge Hognestad, Knut Arne Kummeneje, Tore Nygaardsmoen, Olaf Scheel, and Arnt Inge Vistnes. Finally, I wish to thank Ed Breisacher and The Darwin Press for believing in the project, and for doing an excellent job improving the text and transforming it into a book.

CHAPTER ONE

The Source. From the garden of a former monastery in Bavaria.

The Divine Force

A Source

We humans have always searched for a mythical Force, and the search has not been in vain. A Force has revealed itself by providing a feeling of closeness to an intangible entity revered for having blissful qualities. For many people this revelation is the gateway to a wonderful state of mind. Besides an intense joy, engaging in this entity typically includes a sense of unity with all living creatures; moreover, the entity can serve as a close companion and a dear friend. People like to refer to this mind-capturing source as *Divine,* or simply as *God.* For those who know how to engage, the source can relieve the stress of living, offer guidance through the jungle of life, and cause considerable contentment. It is like a well where the water only rises the more one drinks.

Although the capacity to sense Divinity appears to be laid down in the design of our brains, there will always be those who, for various reasons, close their minds.

––––––

Humanity is moving toward a dark landscape. Around us we are beginning to recognize threatening contours in the form of ecological destruction, war, and famine as well as social and economic breakdown. Some dangers are nearby; more lurk in the distance. We may be able to find paths that avoid many of these obstacles, but others, such as pollution and the draining of resources, seem almost impossible to deal with. We need all the help we can get in order to find, and follow, a navigable course.

Yet, it seems that we are about to turn our back on a phenomenon that may help us. The source we refer to as God can offer a helping hand. Science provides a way for us to *find* a sustainable path, but it is not sufficient to *know* which trail one should follow. We are not that good at making sensible decisions. For example, it does not help to know how to avoid war and environmental destruction if we cannot persuade people to cooperate in implementing solutions.

Religion offers something that is complementary to science: God can impact on the human psyche in a special way, reaching emotions that science is unable to touch. People follow God. To the extent that we are able to comprehend our problems, God can "hold our hands" and lead us down the right path.

————

There are, however, reasons why we should be cautious when drinking from the spring of Divinity. It may be dangerous. We should be careful not to become too inebriated by the holy water, since it is important to retain critical judgment. It is paramount that science be included in our efforts, because science provides the best opportunity for locating a navigable path. We need to apply all our knowledge to ensure that God leads us in the best possible direction.

There are those who work hard to put a lid on the Divine well and prevent people from coming near, the reason being that human history reflects a vast variety of adverse consequences stemming from religious engagement. In order to take full advantage of this source, we need therefore to resolve some issues. We must find a way to handle three problems that together tend to limit the benefits inherent in an otherwise fruitful fountain:

1. Many people not only deny the existence of any form of Divinity, but also try to prevent others from taking advantage of their inner spirituality.
2. Among those who sense God, some end up in trivial and disruptive conflicts over how best to describe the Divine.
3. God can be used for evil purposes, or simply lead us in a wrong direction.

With regard to the first problem, there will always be people who readily form an intimate relationship with God, as there will be those who are unable to sense anything Divine. We need to accept the diversity inherent in the human race; however, never before has Divinity faced an adversary—modern science—that claims to be able to deprive it of all its power.[1]

————

[1] See, for example, Richard Dawkins, *The God Delusion* (2006). Dawkins, formerly a Lecturer and reader in zoology at Oxford University, has been referred to as the "chief gladiator of science" in the battle with religion.

Science-based criticism became obvious during the Age of Enlightenment in the eighteenth century. The main point then, as now, is that society should be based on a rational understanding of reality, and that God is an obstruction to this stance. Divinity is indefinable and as such is undesirable—even more so because many of the historical doctrines stand counter to current science. Certain religions, including Christianity, are particularly vulnerable to scientific criticism. Christians sometimes use the torch of science to illuminate the details of their doctrines, for example, in trying to verify the biblical "Story of Creation." This tends to backfire. The Bible was not written to comply with 21st-century knowledge; thus, defending its content, as if that were the case, is asking for disapproval.

Actually most creeds are under attack, because nearly all religious traditions and writings contain passages that are not in accordance with the present understanding of the world. These texts were written at a time when science, theology, and philosophy were more unified. Two thousand years ago there was no conflict between religion and science because the Bible reflects the understanding of reality available at the time. Theology, however, is conservative by nature, and has therefore failed to revise its teaching according to more recent knowledge.

Science cannot be blown away, but should we simply deny anything religious?

I do not think the focus should be on whether the scientific understanding is correct. In my mind science offers, by definition, the best strategy for describing the world. *That, however, does not mean we need to reject God, because the worldview outlined by science is not in conflict with God's existence, only with some of the myths and dogmas our ancestors once maintained.* In fact, there are many examples proving that even the most rational scientist can sense the Divine source.[2]

---

[2] A well known example is Francis S. Collins, who has written an interesting book about his relationship with God: *The Language of God* (2006). Former director of the National Human Genome Research Institute, he became head of the National Institutes of Health (NIH) in 2009 and was awarded the presidential medal of freedom for his contributions to genetic research.

Painting Portraits

As to the second of the three problems—the question of how best to describe God—it is pertinent to point out that throughout history the Divine has always been presented in different ways. The portraits or depictions of God are made by humans and obviously differ in design. There is nothing wrong with people forming their personal images of God. This is the way it should be. The problem is that the disparities may nourish contention and rivalry.

For our early Stone Age ancestors, differing images were probably not a problem. They interacted primarily with neighboring tribes, which meant people of much the same cultural background. Within these narrow geographical regions Divine spirits were depicted in more or less the same way. Moreover, their portraits were not designed to compete with other presentations. As population density increased, so did territorial disputes. Consequently people were forced to move around, which caused additional conflicts between tribal groups. Eventually the survival of the group became increasingly dependent on size and strength. Religion proved to be a useful tool for uniting larger congregations of people and ensuring a superior command of the community. Thus, the best religions improved survival not only for its adherents but for the creed itself.

There are certain criteria for what makes a belief system end up on the winning side. For one, it helps to draw up a clear distinction between "the true God" and the deities of opponents, and thus between "us" and "them"; two, it helps to evangelize so that as many as possible are included in the "us" group; and three, it helps to have a God that rewards those who fight on the right side. The winners are still with us, but unfortunately the qualities described above are not an advantage when it comes to improving the relationships among creeds.

The present situation is considerably different when compared to the Stone Age world. There is no longer any spare territory to move to, and conflicts are consistently destructive for all parts involved. Mankind would certainly be better off if people focused on what the different creeds share, rather than where they differ. We can and should converge on what lies behind our worship. And instead of using variations in portrayal for political purposes, we should appreciate the cultural richness they reflect. It is not God who creates the problems; it is our attitude toward fellow humans.

People need a depiction of God. They need to imagine what God is like, because it is difficult to engage with an entity that does not have some sort of "face." We need portrayals because they help us drink from the spring, and thereby derive more strength from the Divine source. The question therefore is whether we can create a portrait that is not so easily misused, or lead to conflict with other portraits, or with science. How can we present the Divine in a way that makes it easier for everyone to reach for this source?

A possible starting point is to consider two rather different approaches—two distinct strategies—for the task of portraying God.

One way to form an impression of God is through the stories we tell, the icons and monuments we create, and the mental picture we see with our inner eye. These are all inspired by Divinity, but personal and cultural factors will necessarily influence their appearance. Consequently there is a new belief system in each new culture, and each individual has his or her own way of dealing with the Divine. This is the *personal portrait*.

The alternative is to try to find a more universally valid description—a vision that reflects a mythical force that can be seen as responsible for the world. This implies a description of what may be at the core of Divinity—the essence that is common to all creeds. The most obvious approach is, arguably, to consider God as the Force behind the creation of the Universe and at the same time as a permeating feature of the Universe. I shall make a vague sketch of such a Divine principle, but this *universal presentation* is necessarily indistinct. The sketch lacks vitality; it lacks the color, detail, and energy of the more personal depictions. It is, in other words, deficient in key qualities that are important in order to be a focus of worship.

The point is that both these ways of describing God are useful. They are both important and appropriate because they have a lot to offer mankind. We need the personal portraits in order to develop devotion and to appreciate the Divine presence, and we need the universal presentation to demonstrate that Divinity is not in conflict with science, and to appreciate that all religions revolve around the same entity.[3]

The universal presentation should be consistent with scientific knowledge; however, that does not imply that there is only one possible way of depicting God. There is room for several ways of seeing—and sensing—the Divine within a scientific frame. Moreover, a portrait that is consistent with current science is not necessarily compatible with tomorrow's insight. Most likely we will never have any final version of what the Universe is like, and neither will we find any ultimate description of Divinity. Fortunately, these human limitations of translating reality into words or pictures do not really matter; the personal way to sense, and appreciate, God does not require exact knowledge. The most useful portraits appeal to our emotions, and they serve us independently of any science-based worldview.

———

The way we relate to art can be seen as a parallel to our relationship with God: A painting is not valued for providing the most accurate representation of reality but for the thoughts and perceptions it fosters. A photo offers a more true-to-life representation, but it is within the power of a capable artist to contribute something more. An artist can communicate a novel and enticing way to perceive a person or scenery. People judge paintings based on what the paintings offer them personally; that is to say, what sort of ideas and emotions they foster, not on how accurate the portrayal is. Art entices us in ways that reality cannot.

On the other hand, even abstract paintings presumably reflect a motif based in reality and, at the very least, reality in the form of ideas present within the head of the artist. Paintings are typically inspired by actual objects even though the artist may distort the motif. Similarly, the various portraits of God are based on some-

———

[3] Others have expressed similar ways of thinking. The two ways of portraying the Divine entity are, for example, related to the concepts of private revelations and public revelations as described by Reverend Michael Dowd in *Thank God for Evolution* (2007). Public revelations reflect the scientific view of the Universe, while the private revelations are the personal experiences that people have and on which they base their sense of reality and their engagement with God.

thing real. In both cases—that is, the painter and the writer of religious texts—it is a question of finding inspiration in perceived reality. The motif is out there, indifferent to the colors and lines chosen. As long as one accepts the existence of the Universe there is room for the Divine within our current understanding of reality. Moreover, the elusive quality of the entity referred to as God makes it particularly open for personal interpretation. In fact, since we know next to nothing about the actual features of the Divine, human abstractions are required in order to create any image.

Two artists will never treat a subject in exactly the same fashion. There are many ways to use art for the purpose of stimulating our senses and emotions. Some people admire non-figurative images with bright colors, others prefer more murky or more factual depictions. In the same way that we appreciate diversity in art, we can also appreciate the many different portraits of God. Moreover, rather than complain about perceived inaccuracies, we can try to engage ourselves in the visions presented. Whether it is a painting or a religious icon we have in front of us, only through commitment will they yield meaning and provide gratification.

It is not for all to enjoy art, but it is possible to develop this capacity. It is also possible to develop the ability to sense God.

This book describes possible properties of the Divine entity, but the text does not provide much more than a frame and a canvas. The personal portraits are more important than the attempt at a universal portrait presented here. We benefit from adding individual color and detail to the canvas, as it helps us engage in God. Even if the Divine can be described as a faceless Force, it is better to worship God as an enlightened and sympathetic friend. However, when people of different visions mix and for some reason fail to understand that the details of their portraits are of a personal nature, it may be useful to point out that all the portraits are based on a common Divinity shared by all believers.

Critical voices tend to focus on the imperfections and scientific inaccuracies of the human attempts at describing God. Atheists do not see the authenticity behind the portraits—the deeper qualities—but object to a dubious stroke of the brush or a troublesome choice of color. They disapprove of details that do not reflect the current worldview, or commandments that are out of line with personal opinions. We find similar attitudes in religious people who scrutinize the details of other denominations. (See Appendix I: *Related Portraits*, p. 187).

Spectators are expected to have opinions about works of art, and artists are usually pleased to receive feedback. Likewise, for those who have developed a particular way to sense God, it may be useful to hear comments from other people. But critics should be careful. It is important to remember that both religion and art are sensitive topics because they reflect personal sentiments and profound convictions. Expressed opinions should therefore be constructive and considerate. It is also important to remember that people have different needs and different tastes—both in terms of art and in belief systems. Details that one person disapproves of may very well be of great significance for others.

Hindu deities outside Auroville in India.

To the extent that there is any point in assessing the quality of the various personal portraits of God, an appraisal should primarily be in terms of the impact they have on adherents. The important issue is to what extent the portrait offers benefits to individual believers and to society. Whether the portraits are compatible with scientific theory is really only relevant for those who otherwise would have problems becoming engaged in Divinity.

The universal presentation, on the other hand, should adapt to current science. God is part of reality—at least according to how I use the term here. It is therefore possible to paint a faint portrait consistent with the present view of the world. (In Appendix II: *The True Faces of Reality,* p. 191, I try to add additional substance to a universal presentation of God.) The devotee of science should, however, be aware that current science does not offer a correct model for everything that goes on in the Universe; the future will surely bring a different description of reality. That, however, does not pose any problem, because the universal presentation of God can adapt to changes in our scientific models. In fact, the requirement for compatibility between science and faith is not necessarily that troublesome. *If the Divine power lies in the creation of the Universe, it is reasonable to consider our scientific representation of reality as a constituent in our description of God.*

———

There are a vast number of portraits of the Divine.[4] Humans have also used a variety of names. I choose to use terms such as Divine and Force, but I also refer to the same entity as God. The word "God" is perhaps the more controversial. I use it because this is what Divinity is normally referred to in the Western cultural tradition. There is, however, a strong tendency to associate the name with Christianity or Islam. In this book, God has the wider meaning of being a name for anything that is in the focus of spiritual devotion.

I consider that one can have a personal relationship with God. That does not mean God needs to be viewed as a being or a tangible

———

[4] Anthropological estimates suggest that humans throughout history have created some 100,000 distinct creeds. See A. F. C. Wallace, *Religion: An Anthropological View* (1966). Actually, as each religious person has his or her own way of relating to God, the total number of ways to sense the Divine is limited only by the size of the human population.

creature. Those who prefer to do so may further personalize God—for example, by referring to the Divine as Him or Her. Others may prefer to imagine Divinity as a vague force. It is up to each person to add content. Some like to see God as a living being, perhaps with a human face, while for others it is a question of some sort of "energy." It is also up to the individual to choose different names, such as Gaia, Creator, or Universe. Those who dislike the word "God" may, when reading this text, substitute God with whatever term they prefer.

Renaissance painters liked to depict God as an old man with a grey beard crawling around in the clouds. Personally, I am not surprised that after millions of hours spent peeking out of airplane windows, no one has ever seen such a figure. I disagree, however, with claims that the term "God" cannot correspond to anything real. Other relevant, descriptive words include "ultimate reality," "unified laws of nature," "the story of everything," the "source," or "utmost authority" of the Universe. I consent to all these terms. I can also agree with those who claim that God does not exist—*if the content they add to this word differs from that of the present text.*

Why Pray for God's Presence?

Some atheists claim to know more or less everything that goes on in the Universe and that, upon leaving no stone unturned, there are no traces of God. They also claim that the lack of any tangible signs of spiritual energy implies that no such being or thing exists, and that any alternative stance is meaningless.

The atheist viewpoint is in principal rational: Science does offer the best description of our physical reality, and it is difficult to find God in the light of a scientific torch. Nevertheless, those who sense God's power and beauty know that this light does not shine on everything. It is not a question of looking carefully enough, or of finding hidden corners of the Universe, but a question of knowing *how* to search. One needs a special torch that actually illuminates God's existence.

Those who, in their mind's eye, possess such a torch, feel God's presence in the midst of a rational perception of the world. God is not hiding behind a rock. The Divine power is there right before their eyes, situated in the waves of the oceans, in the flow of the rivers, the beauty of the smallest flowers, and the serenity of the highest mountains. The point is that you may need to close your eyes in order to see, because to perceive God requires awareness rather than comprehension.

If the word "God" is used simply as an alternative name for the Universe, then one is looking straight at God every time one opens one's eyes. A lack of acceptance could be compared to not seeing the forest, but only the trees. For me, God is a bit more than just the visible, material aspect of the Universe. God is an entity that created and permeates everything.

No matter how deep we focus, we will never see an elementary particle; scientific experiments may, nonetheless, convince us that they exist. The presence of a pervasive God can only be conceived through an emotional engagement. You may never stand face to face with God, but you may sense a Divine presence in nature, and you may meet God in your mind.

We typically talk about believing in God, although belief is perhaps not the essential element of faith. The Latin word for religious confession, credo, can be translated as "I give my heart." The term reflects that religiousness is primarily about an emotional engagement; it is about having a personal relationship with God.

It is not necessary to analyze all aspects of a person in order to develop a friendship. In fact, it may not be necessary to know much at all about that person; it is sufficient to feel that he or she is someone one wants to be with. The same can be said about relating to God.

It should be possible to resolve the conflicts involving faith. I believe that a central element of resolution is to assimilate the Divine with current scientific knowledge and at the same time to accept that there are many ways to worship God. In other words, believers may subscribe to the notion that their portraits of God, even if they are inspired by the Divine, are also flavored by human creativity. Atheists may want to accept that, for some people, the term "God" reflects something real. If people agree with these statements, we can perhaps calm the flames that nourish both the disputes among various creeds as well as the discord between science and faith. To this purpose we need a description of the Divine based on current knowledge.

But is this not what all religious scriptures are about? The various prophets described God as best they could. The depictions reflect the knowledge and cultural scaffold of their times, in addition to the prophets' personal ways of sensing God. The story of Divinity has been told again and again a thousand times. It is just that the presentation ought to be updated occasionally.

An updated version is particularly important today as a result of the enormous progress in our understanding of the Universe and life on Earth. Current scientific knowledge implies that some aspects of previous descriptions of God easily fall short, but it also means that we have more information to add. Most religions include interpretations of how the world was created; a well-known example is, of course, the story of Genesis in the Bible. Science has now placed us in a position to outline the Creation in a way that not only is far more detailed but also far more fascinating than the Book of Genesis.[5]

Two thousand years ago, religion and science stood together. The wise men who tried to understand observable phenomenon were involved in both—presumably at the same time. The religious aspects were part of their experience of reality; spirits and other forms of Divinity were an integrated aspect of the insight they used to explain everything from the fate of humans to natural phenomena. Today, scientists and religious devotees belong to two different camps, and between the camps is a deep gap that restricts communication.

Written language is a blessing but also a likely culprit in the present schism between science and religion. As long as the cultural transmission from generation to generation was oral, it was easy to update the ideas expressed, including those of a religious nature. Consequently, novel notions concerning secular matters did not find resistance in the spiritual sphere. Havoc occurred, however, upon the invention of writing. Written statements are much better preserved and consequently less adaptable than their oral counterparts. Moreover, the profession of the priesthood, which was set up to deal

---

[5] See Chapter Three, "The Creation," for a discussion on how we presently understand our Universe.

The Virgin Mary inside a partly ruined building in Portugal.

with spiritual matters, grasped the opportunity to declare the written accounts the primary source of knowledge. As science gained an ever deeper understanding of reality, the gap between the scriptures and the sciences widened. Of course it meant conflict. Following the advances in knowledge beginning in the Renaissance, and the concomitant improved availability of printed books, there are simply too many examples of these conflicts leading to overt combat.

It is a paradox that today, when the conflicts related to religion have made it so difficult to live with God, spirituality may actually be particularly important. Obviously we can survive without religion. We can also survive without art, music, and love. Contrary to the notions of some scientists, most people live happy lives even without any deeper comprehension of science. Still, all these aspects of human endeavor have a lot to offer—religion not the least.

Indeed, several scientific studies conclude that believers have on average better health and happier lives.[6] Moreover, God can be the factor required to avoid the Armageddon the world seems to be heading toward. Based on the capacity to influence the human mind, religion may help us organize humanity so that not only we who are alive today, but also the population of tomorrow, can lead decent lives.

———

As a scientist I can understand why many people refute the existence of God; after all, the traditional religious texts have their limitations. There is, however, another stance taken by many atheists that I find more dubious: Some atheists seem to consider man as a totally rational being. It appears as if they believe humans function somewhat like a computer: It is sufficient to add relevant information about what is good and what is bad, and then press the "enter" button—and *yes*, the outcome is rational behavior.

We humans are not computers. We are biological beings shaped by the process of evolution. This implies that we are equipped with various emotions and innate tendencies, which together have a considerable impact on observed behavior. We have, admittedly, intelligence and a strong dose of free will, more so than any other species; and we can be educated and shaped by society. It is therefore correct to point out that we have the capacity to choose our own actions and that we are open to external pressure, but we are nevertheless influenced in our decisions by various propensities laid down in the genes. In order to help people live wisely and behave nicely, it is therefore useful to employ other means than just pure logic. I believe religion is the most potent tool at hand in this respect.

———

[6] H. G. Koenig, M. E. McCullough, and D. B. Larson, *Handbook of Religion and Health* (2001), offers a comprehensive overview. See also, A. L. Ferriss, "Religion and the Quality of Life," *Journal of Happiness Studies* 3 (2002): 199–215.

Religion offers the possibility of stimulating the human psyche's positive aspects—our compassion and love—and of curbing our inherent egoism and violent tendencies. The opportunity rests in our hands. It is a question of managing the Divine source wisely; that is to say, to encourage the positive features of faith, and avoiding the adverse consequences.

Avoiding the unfortunate outcomes of religious behavior is perhaps the biggest challenge. Even those who are unable to sense God tend to accept that there is strength in faith—that in the concept of Divinity rests a considerable capacity to capture the minds of people. Unfortunately, it is possible to use this source for both good and evil purposes; considerable violence and atrocities have been carried out in the name of God. Although this quandary, which represents the third and last of the aforementioned problems, is difficult to handle, it should not be insurmountable.

Most people, both believers and non-believers, probably agree that there is no such thing as a malicious God. Although several religious texts describe God as an entity responsible for considerable hostility, these references presumably reflect the thoughts of the authors, not deeds performed by any Divine power.[7] After all, the personal portraits reflect human nature, and in humans it is easy to find both good and evil.

It is also important to point out that, although religion can be employed to promote or intensify conflicts, humans are rather adept at killing in the absence of any Divine support. The worst crimes against humanity in the 20th century—Stalin's Soviet Union, Nazi Germany, the Cultural Revolution in China, Pol Pot's Cambodia, and the Hutu-Tutsi conflict in Rwanda—were not based on religious sentiments; that is to say, the perpetrators did not lean heavily on any spiritual ideology to back up the genocides. It is tempting to point out that the religiously driven conflicts of recent history did not escalate to mass murder of the same magnitude.

We take notice when people kill in the name of God, but what about all the killings that did not take place? The murders that

---

[7] Religious texts typically include passages where God displays wrath or encourages combat. Presumably these passages were written for the purpose of persuading people to comply with moral standards, or to gather people together in the face of external threats. In the Bible (KJV: King James Version) you may look up these references: Numbers 31:17–19, most of the book of Joshua, and II Samuel 24:15.

were stopped because various creeds appealed to our compassion for various humans, after all, is the more fundamental component of most creeds. The observation that the worst genocides were committed in the absence of religion does, however, suggest in which direction the net impact of faith has been. Moreover, if one looks at those who donate both money and time to help others, then a religious attitude seems to offer the strongest correlate.[8]

Another oft-cited example is that Christianity is guilty of complicity to slavery in North America. This may be true, but bondage was invented long before the time of Christianity and would certainly have flourished in the absence of any support from the clergy. Moreover, those who put the blame on religion appear to forget that Christian attitudes were also crucial for the movement that managed to abolish slavery.

It is true that religion has been used to defend and maintain dubious practices, but it has also been a vital force in the fight to avoid violence and abolish oppression. Atheists typically pay attention to the former, but not so much to the latter. If we were to judge religion for what has happened throughout human history, it is necessary to have some idea about *what would have been* in the absence of faith. We do not know. But it is far from obvious that journalists and writers of history would have fewer wars and less misery to gorge upon.

In other words, there is no reason to assume that society can avoid violence and tyranny just by burying God—or that the absence of spirituality is the key to kinder citizens. A better strategy is to find, and resolve, the secular causes of conflicts, and to appeal to God for help in implementing possible solutions.

———

There is hardly any doubt that religion can be exploited in connection with war and conflict, but a different aspect of human nature is also often misused in these situations: Our compassion for others is almost as potent a weapon as religion!

War has a lot to do with solidarity among people. Those who lead the soldiers put great emphasis on community spirit: "all for one and one for all." Accordingly, soldiers are willing to risk their lives in order to help others belonging to the same group. Thus, to a large extent their fighting is based on compassion—unfortunately

---

[8] See A. C. Brooks, *Who Really Cares* (2007).

at the expense of people who happen to be on the opposite side of the conflict. Nevertheless, nobody is likely to blame our inherent altruism for the atrocities of war; or claim that we should try to counteract compassion in order to prevent possible misuse of this aspect of human nature. The point here is that both religion and empathy reflect qualities of the mind that have the potential to do much more good than evil. The intention should therefore not be to quell these properties, but to employ them for the purpose of improving society.

Some of the brush strokes in the various portraits of God have proven to be particularly adverse. For example, certain subcultures

The 12th-century Khmer Hindu temple, Angkor Wat, at Angkor, Cambodia, is known as the world's largest religious structure. This religiously harmonious society lasted from A.D. 900 through A.D. 1300.

within Christianity and Islam glorify the idea of dying in war for the sake of God. A similar notion was present in Norse mythology: Valhalla, the Viking version of heaven, was only available for those who died with a weapon in hand. For the head of a state, such attitudes may seem appropriate, as they make people risk their lives for the good of the community; but in a world in dire need of peace, they are dangerous. Fortunately, it is possible to apply some novel brush strokes to the portraits of God for the purpose of altering these attitudes.

It is not possible to change Divinity, but it is possible to influence how people relate to God. In short, we ought to nurture the positive aspects of faith because religion can bring out the best in people—which is why we should pray for God's presence.

CHAPTER TWO

Fishermen navigating toward the sun close to the Island of Zanzibar.

Science and Reality

God

Then it started. At that moment time began to move and the Universe was born—suddenly, from a position apparently containing nothing, yet including everything. In this one point and at this one instant lay the seed of a new world. The source of all matter was there, but packaged in a space without extension, and in a form we are unable to imagine. In this intangible seed was not only substance sufficient for the creation of a complete Universe, but also the physical laws and principles set to govern and thus mold all the strange things to come. Everything was released at this one moment.

What poured out of the spot was a form of energy. It spread at a speed never again to be matched. This energy of unknown character gave rise to substance in the form of *elementary particles*.[1] We call this first moment of time the *Big Bang*; although there was nothing like an explosion, just an expansion faster than the speed of light. Nothing in our experience is suitable to an understanding or depiction of what actually happened in those very first fractions of a second of what we call reality. It is possible to make vague models of the incident, but they fall short of explaining what went on. The only thing we can say for sure is that the opening scene must have been petrifying: The temperature was incredibly high, and so was the density of energy. After only a millionth of a second the cosmos was enormous, and it contained all the mass and energy that today is divided between myriads of galaxies, each with billions of stars. Our planet is less than a drop in the ocean compared to the expanse of the Universe.[2]

Surrounding the seed lay the quantum vacuum as an infinite scene prepared to accept the story about a new era. We are a part of

---

[1] Elementary particles are fundamental building blocks of the Universe of which all physical elements, including the atoms, are built.

[2] The observable Universe began with the Big Bang, but the theory says nothing about what may have preceded this event.

this performance, "the theatre of the cosmos," yet it is a narrative so far-reaching and fantastic that we can only describe minor bits of it.[3]

What we do know is that this first incident meant everything! We are here because a seed was created, and some power, taking the shape of physical laws, ensured that the seed developed into the right kind of Universe. On the face of it, what happened appears to be completely incomprehensible. How can a Universe arise from seemingly nothing? How is it possible to capture all energy and all matter in a point without extension? What was the source of the physical laws that have done such a wonderful job at directing the cosmic theater—that is, orchestrating our Universe?

Yet, of all the questions many scientists and philosophers are struggling to answer, perhaps the most fundamental—and most astounding—is *why?* Why did it all happen? No matter how much knowledge one can provide, and no matter how detailed one understands the Universe, our scientific descriptions do not offer anything in terms of purpose or meaning.

—————

One way of evading this challenge is to simply claim that there is no answer. Whatever happened simply happened. As a scientist this is not an entirely satisfying response, but there is an alternative stance: Something, some entity, stands behind the Creation we refer to as the Universe. That entity is a principle, or a creative power, with qualities that we are unable to comprehend. A Force with characteristics far beyond our capacity to grasp. Thus the Force that gave birth to the Universe has features that, lacking any scientific terms to describe it, may best be represented by the words *Divine* or *God.*

Some atheists dislike these terms. As far as I can see, they are left with two alternatives: Either to leave blank answers to questions

—————

[3] The quantum vacuum is a theoretical construct describing a kind of open scene or platform that the Universe unfolds upon. According to one theory, the scene was there even before the Big Bang, ready to care for an emerging Universe. According to this theory everything that takes place in the Universe are excitations of elementary particles upon the underlying quantum vacuum, somewhat like ripples in an all encompassing sea. The theory fits with the Buddhist notion of a "permanent identity" that is behind everything that exists.

such as those mentioned above about how and why the Universe was established, or devise alternative names for an underlying entity.

Einstein once tackled the quandary with the following statement:

"I'm not an atheist and I don't think I can call myself a pantheist. We are in the position of a little child entering a huge library filled with books in many languages. The child knows someone must have written those books. It does not know how. It does not understand the languages in which they are written. The child dimly suspects a mysterious order in the arrangement of the books but doesn't know what it is. That, it seems to me, is the attitude of even the most intelligent human being toward God." (Quoted by D. Brian, *Einstein: A Life* [1996], p. 186.)

––––––––

The world slowly cooled down. As a consequence, the elementary particles formed matter; they came together in hydrogen atoms. At a much later stage, a variety of atoms were created, and some of them would bind to each other to form molecules, which are the construction units for the more tangible and wonderful parts of our Universe.

The particles gathered in huge clouds, which gradually developed into stars and galaxies. At one point darkness disappeared: When the temperature had dropped sufficiently, it became possible for light to exist. We can still "see" a remnant glow of this first dawn in the sky.[4]

Eons later a creature appeared—man—who fostered a relationship with whatever was accountable for the Creation. Man gave that Force the name God.

––––––––

This is how the story of the Creation begins. The story of how the reality that surrounds us arose. The description reflects the view

––––––––

[4] The remains of the first light are referred to as the cosmic microwave background. These microwaves consist of photons that have wandered the Universe since they were first formed some 380,000 years after the Big Bang. At that point the Universe had cooled sufficiently for electromagnetic particles, that is, photons, which includes light, to exist. For a brief introduction, see R. Cowen, "News of the Early Universe," *Science News* 162 (2002): 390.

Offering the "hand of God."
Child standing on an outdoor altar on the island of Jomfruland, Norway.

of the present-day sages: the men and women of science. Nobody knows all the details, but much of what has happened, and what still takes place, can be explored by anyone with the required curiosity and knowledge to read the scientific scripts. Gradually we have been allowed to comprehend the planet we inhabit and the surrounding cosmos. Our collective wisdom is almost without limits. Although much is still unclear, it is possible to suggest answers to most questions.

Human insight is in itself a marvel almost as incredible as the creation of the Universe. Why do we have this capacity? Do we really need to know? Knowledge of distant galaxies is certainly not required for survival and procreation; our curiosity takes us far beyond the practical tasks associated with living. In fact, it seems as if insights into our nature have proven to be a double-edged sword—our existence has only become more uncertain as a consequence. Knowledge has caused quandaries for us to the point where we are about to lose control and in danger of destroying our basis for existence on this planet. Our intellect may be as much a cause as a solution. Consequently, one of the most exhilarating aspects of the entire story of the Creation is whether human beings will be able to control themselves. A task that may require more than simply scientific knowledge.

There are limits with regard to how far our scientific visions can take us, and how deep our insight can penetrate. Some of the riddles of the Universe will forever rest beyond humankind's capacity to understand. No one may ever know what happened before the beginning of time, or what lies beyond the infinite—not to mention the question of *why* we exist. Science lacks the momentum to analyze seriously these most profound issues.

Although no one *knows*, the strange thing is that there are many who *sense* an answer: The Divine power started the Universe and ensured that it evolved in the direction of a species with the ability to understand what it is all about. This response is not based on traditional science; yet it may be able to supplement our incredible insight into reality. And, more importantly, perhaps the response can help us control what happens on Planet Earth: Religion can complement science when it comes to directing human activity.

———

One of the revelations research has offered us is particularly fascinating: The physical laws of the Universe, and the accompanying physical constants, are required to be extremely fine-tuned in order to allow for the formation of solar systems with planets, for the formation of life based on organic chemistry and, not the least, to allow for the appearance of human beings. Only minor discrepancies in the laws that govern the Universe would have resulted in a cosmos where neither planets nor life can exist. This realization has been referred to as *the anthropic cosmological principle.*[5]

If, for example, the force of gravity had been stronger, the Earth would be pulled into the sun. On the other hand, if the force was

———

[5] The most famous outline of this principle was written by J. D. Barrow, F. J. Tipler, and J. A. Wheeler, *The Anthropic Cosmological Principle* (1988). For more recent presentations, see B. Bryson, *A Short History of Nearly Everything* (2005), or J. D. Barrow, *The Constants of Nature* (2003).

less powerful, the Earth would be cast into space, and thereby lose its life-giving connection with the sun. The laws governing the relationship between elementary particles offer another example: Their design allows for the assembly of atoms of varying size and property, including the specific atoms that life on Earth is made of. Moreover, these atoms, particularly carbon, ended up with a set of peculiar properties that are crucial for the development of living organisms. It seems as if the laws of physics are not just incidentally consistent with biological evolution, but that they were designed for such an event to occur.

The story of life is like a fairytale. We refer to the process responsible as *evolution*, but this process is an integral part of something that began with the creation of the Universe. Evolution was made possible by the particular chemical laws of nature, which again are just reflections of the fundamental physical properties of the cosmos. Evolution directs organic development toward life with ever-increasing complexity—including more advanced nervous systems and, concomitantly, improved intellect. In other words, the opportunity to have a creature with the ability to understand was laid down in the development of our species. More importantly, the physical laws appear to be fine-tuned toward this aim. (See *Evolution—God's Tool?*, below.)

Evolution—God's Tool?

Evolution is the process that brought life to Earth, beginning with the first, basic unicellular organisms, and continuing onward all the way to mankind and the biological diversity surrounding us. Evolution is based on two rather simple principles: The first is to produce a *variety* of individuals within a species. Biological features are defined by the genes; thus, variety can be obtained by generating changes in the form of mutations in the genes. The genes offer a blue-print as to what sort of properties the organism carrying them will have: If the blueprints differ, then the individuals will differ. The second principle is what we refer to as *selection*—the individuals that have been bestowed with the best genes survive and multiply, whereas the others simply disappear.

The consequence of having these two principles operate is that we become increasingly improved as a species of organisms; the term "improved" implies that our species survives better when facing the challenges of the environment in which we live. In short, natural selection.

There is an inherent tendency in this process to create ever more advanced life forms, but that does not mean perfect adaptations. Survival and procreation is the aim; perfection is neither required nor feasible. Thus, one should not expect that the various species alive today, including us, are flawless. Yet, evolution has been a huge success. Earth has several hundred million living species, and they have adapted to living almost anywhere—from glaciers to hot springs, from cracks deep down in the crust to the air above us.

In popular presentations of evolution, it is common to use expressions such as "the genes prefer" or "it is in the interest of the genes." This is just a simplified way to say something about how evolution has shaped the genes. Obviously, the genes themselves have no opinions or wishes.

On the other hand, you may ask whether there is a purpose to the whole process. Is there a reason why the physical qualities of the Universe allow life to happen, and is it inherent that evolution should move toward a species with the intelligence required to understand what it is all about? The process of evolution is a consequence of the qualities of our Universe. If one considers the Universe to spring out of an entity referred to as God, then it seems fair to consider evolution as a tool devised by this entity. And it is tempting to imagine that the tool was included in the repertoire of processes allowed for because it would lead to a species with the capacity to sense the Creator.

The above observation offers a kind of meaning to our existence: Are we born to be a participating and observing part of the Universe?

In the development of our species, evolution also included a capacity to sense the presence of a "supernatural power"—a Force that stands above us and unites all creatures and features of the cosmos. God is the preferred word used to describe the focus of this awareness.[6]

---

[6] To learn more about the parts of the brain that are active when engaged in religious experiences, see B. Holmes, "In Search of God," *New Scientist* (April 21, 2001): 24–28; or A. Newberg, E. d'Aquili, and V. Rause, *Why God Won't Go Away* (2001).

Standing on the water—with the help of a rock.
Off the island of Jomfruland, Norway.

The Universe did not need any planet harboring life, and mankind could have survived without this particular capacity. Yet, the miracle happened. It is tempting to believe that God wanted someone to relate to, someone capable of understanding the Creation.

———

The path leading from the Big Bang to the presence of human beings depended not only on peculiar physical laws of nature, but also on a long list of surprising events, as will be detailed in Chapter Three: *The Creation*. Some may argue that it is best to regard reality as a series of coincidences; they point out that no matter how small the likelihood may be that conditions in the Universe should be right for life, the probability cannot be zero. If everything is based on randomness—that is to say, our existence reflects solely fluky circumstances—then the presence of an underlying creative Force seems less likely.

Although there is no final answer about how one should relate to reality, the notion that our existence is based on an enormous number of lucky throws of dice seems implausible. The Universe could have remained a homogenous soup of elementary particles. The Universe did not even need to exist. The more we learn and understand how fantastic and extremely complicated the Universe is, the harder it is to imagine that all the required fine-tuning actually is no more than a series of random events. Conversely, the more likely is the presence of an underlying power, or some form of Divine Providence.

Einstein had similar thoughts when suggesting that a limited insight into nature may lead one away from God, while a deeper insight will move one toward God. Moreover, he did not like the thought that nature should be based on some element of chance, and thus stated: "God does not play dice."

So did God, or whatever name one may wish to call the forces behind the Universe, create the world for a purpose?

The associations fostered by the concept of *purpose* are probably not adequate, since it is a term designed for human affairs, and what stands behind the Creation is much grander, more incredible than our thoughts can imagine. The best one can do is to gather all aspects related to a creative entity—whether discernible, unidentified or indescribable—into a single concept: God. There is no way of telling what this concept actually entails; but the lack of definition does not mean a lack of existence; it simply implies that science is unable to outline the exact nature of the concept.

Some may think the word "God" is too pretentious or pompous to be used for an abstract entity that one actually knows next to nothing about. Personally I find it appropriate to use this word, but the choice is trivial; any name would do. God is simply a name chosen by people who like to venerate this entity, and for the purpose of veneration it does not matter that no one is able to provide an accurate, scientific description.

Humans have an inherent tendency to submit to leaders and to regard them with adoration. Musicians, sports heroes, and other celebrities do not need to perform grand miracles in order to be praised almost like gods. It seems natural to venerate an entity that is responsible for our existence. The concept of God is useful for this purpose.

Mankind

It took 13.7 billion years for humans to become a part of the performance referred to as the Universe. Our arrival was unexpected and had dramatic consequences. Modern man (biologically speaking) first appeared some 200,000 years ago, but until quite recently, there was little indication that humans would be able to gain a deeper understanding of reality, or be able to change the face of this planet. Life on Earth had existed for nearly four billion years without evidence of organisms with these capacities.

Of the millions of species that have arisen on Earth, only we humans are capable of seeing beyond the horizon of our existence. We alone have been given the key to understand what the world is about, and the key to form our future. What has happened within historical times is exceptional, surprising, and frightening. Is it ultimately laid down in the Creation that we should be here? For what would be the value of a Universe without someone with the ability to perceive it? And is the intention that we shall not only see and understand, but also participate and care about what is happening?

With the help of science one is able to model the development of the Universe step by step and to formulate ideas about how life arose on Earth, and how the evolutionary process led to ever more advanced organisms. Many of the details are misty, but one can offer an account, albeit vague, of the whole cascade of events. We have, in other words, been given the ability to understand what a momentous wonder the Universe is—a miracle so special and so fantastic that it is almost inconceivable. Moreover, it is within us to sense that some sort of Force is breathing life and energy into the Creation. This entity not only permeates everything, but it unites the whole by being a shared overarching code. All life forms on the planet share the same molecular principles of life; and our planet shares the nature of elementary particles and atoms with all other celestial bodies.

───────

Our intellect is a blessing that has opened many doors. Not only can we understand the machinery of the Universe, but we have also been able to create our own fantastic machines, cure diseases, transform energy to suit our various needs, and walk on the moon. Unfortunately, it is possible that our intellect can also be our enemy. It has given us the opportunity to live a life of comfort, but it has also given us the capacity to destroy the foundation for our own existence—not to mention that of many other species.

It is therefore important to be critical about how to use our knowledge. We must look ahead, far ahead, and carefully consider our actions. It is important that we try to predict the consequences of the many choices we make. In order to find the best route forward, it is necessary to exploit opportunities, but also to realize our limitations. We are not almighty. Maybe we *are* special, yet we are mere creatures shaped like all other living organisms by the process of evolution. We may consider this process a reflection of something Divine; nevertheless, it has its limitations. Evolution has given us both our strengths and weaknesses. We have a fantastic capacity for logical thinking, but also a wide range of emotions and innate tendencies that we cannot easily escape—and that at times can be quite destructive. Putting a man on the moon is the easy task, the hard part is dealing with human nature.

Sometimes we get lost. Maybe we stare for too long into the magic crystal ball we call science. It is easy to lose direction, and let inventiveness lead us down wild roads, especially when technology creates more destruction to the environment than benefits to those who live there.

It is important to understand the consequences of our actions, but unfortunately this understanding is not sufficient. It does not help to realize that we are moving in the wrong direction if we are unable to maneuver down a better path. Our power of influence ultimately depends on our ability to touch people's feelings. In order to do so we need to understand the human mind. Although insight into the inherent nature of mankind is essential, even that is not actually enough. Knowledge alone does not automatically bring out the best in us. We need to find something that can stimulate our finest qualities—something with the power required to lift us up. The human ability to sense the Divine offers an opportunity we can hardly afford to miss.

The most important wisdom is to know ourselves, and the most important revelation is to sense that entity we refer to as God.

The Scientific Point of View

Modern science contributes toward weakening our spiritual propensity, but contrary to popular belief this is not because the concept of Divinity needs to conflict with a scientific worldview. Most controversies concern particular details. Science points its finger at possible "mistakes"—for example, the Biblical idea that the Universe was created a few thousand years ago—but in the process tends to strike at all aspects of religiosity. Opponents associate religion with inappropriate ideas or unwholesome practices, but the concrete aspects criticized are typically associated exclusively with certain creeds—not all religious systems. Moreover, they criticize stories that stand contrary to current science, without considering whether these tales may serve the believer. After all, most people would agree that irrational sensation can in fact serve humans rather well, for example when falling in love. In short, atheists may tend to take a stance against any form of spirituality without first considering whether the critique is relevant for all creeds, or whether the ideas they dislike may actually have a net positive impact on humanity. It may appear as if some people are trying to sacrifice God on the altar of science.

In order to save our relationship to God I need to present the Divine in a way that retains its dignity, but at the same time can withstand scientific scrutiny. That is to say, I need to depict God in a manner that is consistent with our understanding of the Universe, but the presentation should also provide fertile ground for a spiritual relationship. This book attempts to provide such a presentation. The text describes a principle, or power, that is behind the formation of the Universe, and thus also behind the evolution of life on Earth. It is possible to envision God as either being this Force or being responsible for it. These descriptions are merely variations on a common theme. The bottom line is that the Divine entity is in a way responsible for the Universe. It is thus reasonable to argue that the physical and biological guidelines orchestrating reality reflect this Divine power. There is a saying that a mother is present in her child. In a similar manner, we may state that God is present in the stars and planets as well as in the living beings inhabiting them—including us.

Throughout history, there have been several attempts at portraying God in ways comparable to what is presented here. (In Ap-

A chapel in Portugal on the edge of a cliff,
with apparent underground creatures.

pendix I: *Related Portraits*, p. 187, I have briefly described some of
these.) Although it is hardly possible to refute the present notion of
God, it is possible to offer critical comments. In an attempt to meet
the criticism, I shall take a closer look at the relationship between
religion and science.

Humans do not have any definite answer as to how the Divine
should be explained. One reason is that we have insufficient knowledge about the entity we choose to refer to as God; another reason is
that, even if we had known God's true qualities, it would still presumably not be a single answer about how to translate that knowledge into words. In fact, many aspects of reality are too complex to
lend themselves to textual brushstrokes.

An accurate portrayal of God is a mission impossible. Human
language evolved for the purpose of representing human concerns,

Bells belonging to a Portuguese church.

such as our emotions, our experiences, and our everyday affairs. It is no wonder that language often falls short when it comes to the entity referred to as God. Neither are we able to offer a single, unified, and complete description of the Universe, and this is partly due to a lack of knowledge and partly a lack of words. We struggle to depict even something as small and apparently simple as elementary particles. For example, in order to characterize the properties of the particles referred to as quarks, we use terms such as "charm" and "strange," although the normal content of these terms has nothing to do with the actual properties of quarks. Our language simply lacks words that fit.[7]

God is infinitely grander, more difficult to comprehend, and further removed from the human linguistic capacity.

---

[7] There are several popular presentations of quarks and other elementary particles. For those who prefer a version on paper, see B. Greene, *The Fabric of the Cosmos: Space, Time and The Texture of Reality* (2005).

As already mentioned, God's existence is primarily a semantic issue. It depends on what one chooses to mean when using this concept. If you associate God with the Universe, there should be no further need to prove God's existence. I envision God as something more than just an alternative term for the world, and I like to include the impetus that started it all, a power that permeates the Universe and, perhaps, a force with some capacity to intervene or direct later stages of reality. Is it possible to substantiate and defend this expanded concept of God against the zeal of science?

There are probably not that many ardent "crusaders" fighting religion; however, a large number of people are skeptical about the existence of any form of Divine entity, and even more so toward the ways in which humans relate to God. It is estimated that 16% of the current world population is not associated with any form of belief system. At the same time, it is evident that, even in an era characterized by scientific thought, the vast majority agrees that there is some sort of power or principle that may be referred to as Divine. In the country regarded as the stronghold of science, the United States, approximately one half of the scientific community has retained the ability to sense God's presence.[8]

Einstein once said that "the most incomprehensible thing about the world is that it is comprehensible." It is far from obvious that the Universe should be set up in a logical way with definable properties, or that we should be equipped with the intellect required to describe these properties. We may be able to offer a kind of explanation for the processes that take place in the Universe, but the deeper we delve into the details the more amazing is what we find. At the deepest level we encounter the more profound riddles such as: Is there a reason why the Universe exists, and why are we here?

Science is based on asking questions of "why" and "how"; nevertheless, these questions are almost taboo. True, it is difficult, probably impossible, to find methods that provide scientific answers, but I can propose a hypothesis—namely that the world reflects the existence of a Divine entity—and in the absence of any alternative way of responding, this seems to be a rational stance. As a scientist I will

---

[8] The best and most updated overview of world religions can be found at http://www.adherents.com. The article "Scientists and religion in America," *Scientific American* (September 1999): 78–83, covers the situation in the United States.

Burning of incense in a Buddhist monastery, Shanxi province, China.

defend the right to ask any question, whether or not a scientific approach is likely to find a solution. And I tend to prefer a fragile answer, one that may not be well substantiated, rather than no answer. It is normal procedure to create vague models pertaining to unchartered territories, and then at a later point either to reject or advance the models.

In any conflict, the opposing parties tend to polarize. Both sides get stuck in the effort of winning a battle or a debate—rather than listening and evaluating with an open mind the information supplied by the opponent. The conflict between science and religion seems to be no exception. I would hope that open-minded individuals in both camps might accept the perspective presented here: In short, although not all presentations of God fit into the realms of science, God fits into my reality.

Most attacks on God have been directed at the tales and doctrines of particular denominations. The Biblical description of how God created the world is, for example, unprotected cannon fodder for the crusaders of science. Such descriptions are easy to tear down, but in battering God, they appear as if they are attacking windmills.[9] God looms behind these descriptions—not in them. Divinity does not disappear even if you manage to blow up all the statues and burn all the images that people have created. Some critical voices have recognized the above quandary, and directed their assault against the underlying notion of a Divine power. These assaults are the ones more relevant to discuss here. First, however, I have some comments about the more commonly heard critique.

Criticism related to the various details of specific religions can be both justified and constructive. When religious opinions stand in the way of common sense, and thereby obstruct constructive efforts to improve society, it may be appropriate to raise a voice. For example, denying the process of evolution may counteract efforts aimed at improving healthcare. The notion that heaven opens its doors for those who kill in the name of God is used to nourish war. Such examples stand as obvious arguments in favor of neutralizing religious concepts that can damage society, and point out that it is desirable to have a religion that embraces criticism.

On the other hand, it is unnecessary to attack people's personal images of God when these images do no harm to others. We should be able to accept that some individuals choose to believe that God created the Earth in six days. No person, including a scientist, is completely rational in all thoughts and deeds. Even the most hardcore atheist typically "believes" in such notions as human rights and moral values—even if these notions do not necessarily follow from empirical science any more than does the Bible's account of creation. In short, most people prefer to acknowledge ideas that stand without any firm foundation in science. It is tempting to suggest that those who do not tolerate any irrational perception in others are advised to limit their social commitment to computers.

---

[9] The fictional character Don Quixote (in the book *Don Quixote de la Mancha*, by Miguel de Cervantes, 1605) fought windmills because he considered them to be vicious giants. Attacking God's existence on the basis of human constructs, such as the book of Genesis, is, in my mind, similarly misguided.

Attacks on the underlying and indescribable Divine Force are also understandable—and potentially constructive. They may prevent someone from relating to God, but at the same time they can facilitate efforts toward better ways of describing the spiritual aspects of the Universe.

Furthermore, science has a lot to offer mankind, and good science requires an inclination to view everything in a critical light. We need the human capacity to scrutinize and analyze, because we need what science can bring us—in terms of medical treatment, for example. It is only natural that religion also finds itself in the spotlight, and I shall argue why God survives the critical light of science.

It is important to be aware that science is not about proving or disproving anything in a mathematical sense, but rather about building models that describe reality as accurately as present data allows. The quality of these models is measured according to how well they explain our observations and experiments. It is possible to create models that present the Universe without adding any Divinity, but it is also possible to argue that including such an entity will tend to improve the explanations.[10]

In other words, it is not a question of proving or disproving God's existence. The absence of favoring evidence has limited value as evidence for claims that God does not exist—at least in the case of the vague Divine entity outlined in this discussion. Scientifically speaking, it is rather a question of which of two opposing models, the one that includes Divinity and the one that does not, seems more correct and more complete. Thus, the issue is not so much whether the present portrayal of God is compatible with science, but whether it adds anything to our view of the world.

Possibly the most relevant argument against the existence of a Divine force is based on a principle known as Occam's Razor, named after the medieval philosopher William of Occam. It is a KISS (Keep It Simple, Stupid) principle: You shall not create a scientific model that complicates matters beyond what is needed to ex-

---

[10] Some people think of science as a method for describing our *physical* reality, leaving out the spiritual aspects of life. Personally I prefer to deal with only one model of reality in which both physical and spiritual aspects are included. The difference between these two positions, however, may be mostly semantic.

plain the underlying observations. In other words, one ought to "shave off" any embellishments that are not required. The principle can be used to argue that the introduction of Divinity is an unnecessary complication of the scientific description of the world. Put another way: God does not add anything to our understanding of the Universe.

Occam's principle is at best a rule of thumb. There are examples of theories that at the time seemed to be unnecessarily complex, but later proved to be the more accurate description. For Medieval scientists a flat Earth offered the more straightforward explanation for available observations, because, after all, it looks rather flat. Today this model is considered ridiculous. I shall argue that based on current scientific knowledge, there is no need to shave off God; that is, our model of the Universe is not improved by excluding Divinity, but may actually stand to gain, if ever so little, by including the Divine. By adding this entity we obtain in a way a more complete treatment of reality. For example, it does suggest a sort of answer to the question of why the Universe came about and why we are here.

Science is unable to fill in all the answers to the questions we ask. In fact, in the case of certain key issues it can hardly respond at all, such as: What was before the beginning, and *why* does the Universe have the properties required to evolve advanced forms of life. Science also has problems filling in many of the unchartered areas that still exist on our map of the more accessible issues concerning reality. Some of the more problematic topics will be discussed in the next chapter, "The Creation."

What I suggest is that certain subjects may be better dealt with in a model that allows for an underlying Divine principle. The contribution to our explanatory capabilities may be limited, but the model that includes a Divine power does offer a shade of color, or vague strokes of a brush, where present science falls short: The Divine was there before the beginning and is in a way responsible for the Creation. The very peculiar properties of Planet Earth are there to allow for living organisms. The process of evolution aims toward higher complexity so that the Universe will have a Being capable of sensing what it is all about. Although the model that includes God may not be more useful for scientific endeavor, neither should it in any way hamper science. In this respect it is as appropriate as purely secular approaches. In other words, introducing God has limited ex-

An icon and a balance scale in an orthodox monastery
on the island of Skopolos, Greece.

planatory value concerning most of the events we are studying, but
it offers a reasonable, and perhaps more comprehensive, model. It
does not add detailed answers as to what existed before the beginning, but by claiming that God has always been there, the need for
an alternative answer is less importunate. It seems somewhat easier
to envision that a non-physical entity such as God can exist independently of time and space.

As pointed out above, present scientific models have considerable gaps both in terms of the development of the Universe and the
evolution of life on Earth. Although we can explain how the chemical building blocks of life arose, it is very difficult to imagine how
these chemicals managed to unite and become the first living cells.
Scientifically speaking, this event seems highly unlikely; nevertheless, it happened relatively soon after an opportunity for life
emerged on Earth. Envisioning the influence of a Divine power does
not clarify our models regarding the origins of life, but it allows for
an interpretation of why this seemingly unlikely event occurred.

In future, mankind may find rational explanations that cover many of the unchartered areas on our current map. Other areas may remain as silent witnesses of a force with a potential to operate outside our scientific calculations. Even if we are able to explain all the weird things that have happened, both on our planet and in the rest of the Universe, this does not rule out the idea that there is a guiding principle behind it all. There is still room for a vague underlying entity. The existence of a Creator does not depend on having unanswered questions about the Creation.[11]

Scientific understanding of the world has changed dramatically over the last centuries. Gradually we realized that the Earth is just one of several planets circling the sun. We learned about how the evolutionary process forms all living things. We found other galaxies, and we described the particles and forces composing the Universe. Science is innovative, but at the same time somewhat conservative. In every era there is a tendency for people to focus on current explanations of reality. Most people, scientists or laymen, tend to be skeptical toward novel ideas. It took, for example, considerable time for the ideas of Newton and Darwin to win acceptance among a broader audience. True, religious sentiments may be more conservative than scientific worldviews, or for that matter most other aspects of human culture, but a preference for existing dogmas seems to be a distinctive human trait.

The atheistic viewpoint stands strong among present scientists. The question is how solid the atheist foundation really is—when scrutinized with an open and critical eye. Is it really obvious that the only complete way to describe the Universe is like an enormous collection of elementary particles that emerged from nowhere? Or are there additional aspects and properties required in order to complete the description?

Not too long ago, both science and church insisted that the Earth is the midpoint of the Universe, and that man has nothing in common with the animals. In those days, the conservative nature of society made it problematic to describe the world without taking the word of the Bible into account. Today the pendulum seems to

---

[11] Those interested in unchartered areas in our current world "map" may look up "13 things that do not make sense" by Michael Brooks, *New Scientist* (March 19, 2005).

have swung in the opposite direction: It is awkward to suggest a model of the Universe that does include reference to Divinity. I think a good scientist shows humility for the limitations inherent in our quest to understand, and I would not be surprised if the majority of scientists at some point in the future accept a model of the Universe that includes an entity that may be referred to as God. The present dislike for the concept of God seems to be a consequence of the particular conflict between Christianity and science. This conflict has shaped a substantial subculture of both scientists and laymen in the United States, but is hardly noticeable in many other parts of the world.

Science develops theories for phenomenon that we are unable to witness or experience directly. No one has ever seen a proton or a protein, but we have solid evidence as to their existence. That is, the theories that describe them provide the best explanation for the results of various experiments we perform. The mere existence of the Universe, and all the wonders included therein, provides a basis for postulating the existence of something Divine.

Fair enough, the topic of God is difficult and related to an enigmatic side of reality. For many, the immediate response and the simplest answer may be: "no such thing." As Winston Churchill once said: "All complicated questions have a simple answer. Unfortunately, the answer is always wrong."

––––––––

The Holy Grail of science is to develop a theory that ties together all the physical laws operating in the Universe. This Grail has been referred to as the *Grand Unified Theory*, or just GUT for short. The physicist Stephen Hawking has suggested that if we are able to set up such a model for our world, including a complete understanding of the forces of nature, we will have a description of God's soul.[12]

Hawking's notion fits well with the paradigm that the Universe is the "body" of God, and the principles guiding that body are its soul. The description reflects, of course, a tendency to add human characteristics to our vision of God. One may argue that God is far too intangible and indefinable to entail anything resembling either

––––––––

[12] S. Hawking wrote about God's soul in his book, *A Brief History of Time* (1998).

a body or a soul. Moreover, the human soul is a difficult concept to apprehend. We may have ideas about what the word "soul" means, but even if we managed to describe each molecule in the body, we would not have any clear description of what the soul really consists of. Similarly, even if we can provide a unifying description of the laws of physics, we will still be short of a complete rendering of what God is. God seems to be something more than the sum of elementary particles and laws of nature. Although the above brush strokes added to the portrait may be relevant, a complete portrait is likely to be beyond our conceptual capacity.

We can make an exact photographic image of a face, but it is equally beyond our capacity, whether we use language or paint, to give an accurate description of the personality reflected in the face. Yet it is easier to paint a good portrait if one gets to know the person. Although an understanding of natural laws does not provide complete insight into the Divine, such knowledge may enable us to come closer to God.

It is in human nature to desire explanations—whether substantiated or not—but we also have in us a natural skepticism. This combination gives us the ability to believe almost anything, but also to deny even the most rational presentations. It is natural to ask whether there is any God, and if we believe the answer is yes, we want to know what God is like. But as long as nobody knows for sure the true face of God, each person should be allowed to form his or her own image in the same way that one forms a personal impression of someone one is fond of.

————

The strongest arguments for God's existence may be found inside ourselves. In biological terms we are apes who happened to lose our fur. There are, however, aspects of human nature that suggest we are something more, that evolution made an unprecedented leap when shaping humans, that we were given characteristics that distinguish us from all other organisms. These properties are not incompatible with how the evolutionary process operates, but they are so special, so biologically surprising, that it is reasonable to wonder whether there could be something more at work than just random mutations. The main properties I have in mind are our intellect, our capacity for compassion and morality, our self-consciousness, and our ability to sense something Divine.

Current knowledge of the evolutionary process makes it possible to offer a vague description of what happened over the last five million years, during which time our ancestors evolved from apes to humans, but this description does not resolve the presumption that what happened was totally unprecedented and astounding. If a biologist from another planet had appeared on Earth five million years ago, that person would hardly guess that an organism with our properties would emerge. We tend to take our capabilities for granted, but they represent both a surprising and wonderful nudge of the evolutionary process. It is therefore tempting to imagine Divine guidance behind what happened. Perhaps the Divine is incapable of direct intervention in shaping the human mind, but it may still be responsible for the design of the natural laws that made human evolution possible.

———

The prominent position of science in our society is, in my mind, an argument in favor of incorporating the concept of God into the scientific models of reality. I believe this is possible, but I also believe that it is not required for the purpose of engaging God. God is not very suitable as a scientific target. Religion and science are independent entities, and thrive best when living separate lives in the human mind. The problem is not that the two necessarily end up in conflict if combined. God, as presented here, is compatible with current science—at least that is the way I see it. Thus, one need not deny knowledge in order to find room for faith. The point is that God's place in the Universe lies beyond the reach of our scientific methods. The two, religion and science, have more to offer us if we allow them to occupy separate "niches." While science is best served by a rational and non-emotional approach, other aspects of the mind should be engaged when seeking God. That is to say, even though both religion and science are about believing in something, it is a question of two different ways to use the word "believe." Actually, it is about two completely different ways to use your brain. Science is about constructing models based on empirical research and observations. In order to find God you must employ passion.

The philosophers of antiquity saw two different approaches aimed at grasping reality. Plato referred to them as *mythos* and *logos*. The two were considered equally valid. *Logos* (reason and science) was suitable for elucidating material reality, while *mythos* outlined the more mysterious and spiritual aspects of human existence.

It is, of course, possible to ignore any spiritual encounters—in the same way that you can choose to forgo love or not to listen to music. The point is that most of us benefit from engaging not only the intellectual, but also the spiritual, the aesthetic, and the emotional aspects of being human. The brain has an enormous potential and a range of properties that are working side by side; they all serve us in different ways. For example, when you play tennis, you use other parts of the brain than if you are studying biology. Most people would agree that there is no conflict between engaging in sports and studying natural sciences. The point is that these activities do not need to be in conflict with spiritual involvement either. The various activities—sports, science, and religion—are simply cared for by different brain modules.

It is possible to improve our skills in sports and science; we can also improve our spiritual sensitivity. In most forms of sport, it is important to develop the capacity of the subconscious part of the brain to provide optimal control of muscles. Science is about expanding our comprehension about how the Universe works. Religion, on the other hand, is about expressing one's devotion in order to sense and enjoy God's presence.

God's Attributes

I have argued that God has a place not only in the human mind, but also in the Universe. The next big question is to what extent we can outline God's attributes. Did God just put the scene in motion, or does God have the power to intervene? Was creation a creative event, or is it a creative process? And, if it is possible for God to "stretch out the hand" and touch the Creation, in what way and with what capacity?

Most Christians envision an active God with the ability to help people. Deists, however, believe God created the world, but has not been active since then. The Deists paint a minimalist portrait of God—a version that includes a Divine force in the realms of the Universe, but as a rather faceless force.[13]

I believe the question about the power inherent in the Divine is another of the enigmas that lie beyond human ability to resolve; yet

---

[13] T. Paine, *Age of Reason, Being an Investigation of True and Fabulous Theology* (originally published in 1794 [Part I] and 1796 [Part II]).

there are some indications that provide a basis for opinions. And even if we cannot confirm that there is a Divine Force with the capacity to affect the passage of time—a God that looks after the inhabitants of the Universe—it is up to each of us to include these properties in our personal portrait of God.

————

One source for speculation as to God's attributes is to ask whether the development of the Universe was put on an unwavering track right from the start. Is everything predetermined, or can events be affected, albeit in small and insignificant ways, by forces or players that operate within the Universe? If the latter is true, it is possible to consider the impact as an influence originating from the Divine.

The answer to these questions seems to be in favor of non-determinism. For example, the current model of the Big Bang suggests that at the very beginning the physical laws differed from those that apply today. Furthermore, even the current laws may be obsolete when matter is caught up in what we refer to as black holes.[14] The evolutionary process forming life is full of surprises, which may reflect the meddling of a Divine power (to be discussed in the next chapter). These arguments, however, only allow for a conditional "yes" to such an influence because the examples may be interpreted as odd reflections of laws laid down from the beginning.

Perhaps the strongest argument suggesting some flexibility is that we humans actually have the capacity to influence events in a way that could hardly be predetermined at the beginning of time. We have a considerable dose of free will. We can use our free will to deliberately change history, at least as it plays out on our planet. As human capacities are consequences of evolution, our free will offers substance to the idea that God, using us as mediators, has an opportunity to influence. It is tempting to take this idea one step further: Perhaps *we are* God's hand. Perhaps the evolutionary process was established for the purpose of creating such a player.

————

————

[14] Black holes are presumably formed when giant stars collapse. Matter is condensed to extreme densities, causing a gravitational force so strong that even the photons constituting light are retained; consequently, the entities appear to be black. See: C. Barcelo, S. Liberati, S. Sonego, and M. Visser, "Black Stars, not Holes," *Scientific American* (October 2009): 20–27.

The "country" of Damanhur, a spiritual community in Northern Italy.

If the Divine has the capacity to exert authority, the next big question is: Are we are dealing with a benign, neutral, or a malignant power?

It seems easy to argue that the creation of the Universe is not consistent with a malicious Creator. On the other hand, based on human predicaments and the prospect of a bleak destiny, a caring and intervening God is not that obvious either. A more appropriate starting point may be to realize that whether it is an animal or a God we want to characterize, we have this tendency to add human attributes to our descriptions. We like to *anthropomorphize*, that is, to think about any entity or creature we care about as "human-like." That goes for our pet animals—and for our relationship to whatever we consider Divine. Adjectives like good and bad are probably about as irrelevant in the description of God as in the description of flowers or bacteria. God is far beyond those kinds of concepts. The Divine power is a supreme principle with qualities of an entirely different type than what evolution has incorporated into the human brain. Yet, it seems natural to view the Force behind our very existence with positive eyes. It is difficult to consider life as springing from a non-benevolent power.

The above viewpoint entails a problem in the form of the following quandary: If God is good, why do people suffer so much? Should not everyone be kind and happy in a Universe created by a well-intentioned spirit?

One possible answer is that Divine influence does not necessarily imply that God is omnipotent with regard to the affairs taking place in the world. Right from the beginning there may have been limitations inherent in the Creation. For instance, there may have been limitations embedded in the evolutionary process, which restrict what sort of life forms can evolve. We know that evolution does not create perfect organisms. Genes develop qualities that are sufficient to survive and procreate—nothing more. In fact, often less: Most of the species that once roamed the Earth are now extinct. No organism is immune to sickness. Indeed, we humans have a long list of weak points: We are struggling with a poorly constructed spine, a propensity for depression, and an unfortunate tendency to display anger and aggression.[15]

The process of evolution is not capable of creating ideal and flawless animals. Ambition and concomitant aggression come as a consequence of the "struggle for existence." That is, individuals who do not in some way exert themselves will lose in the evolutionary contest. The rules governing evolution depend ultimately on the physical and chemical laws of the Universe. These may again be restricted by principles we do not recognize. The Universe depends on having a set of rules to operate by, and it is very difficult to imagine laws of nature that do not constitute limitations as to what is possible to achieve. In other words, it seems almost unfeasible to have a reality with intelligent life, without aspects of life that are unfortunate for the individual.

———

Many people prefer to see God as an active and sympathetic force; however, both the choice of the term God and the choice of adding particular qualities are personal preferences. God's attributes

---

[15] G. Marcu and H. Mifflin describe in their book, *Kluge: The Haphazard Construction of the Human Mind* (2008), the brain as an organ kept in functional order by the equivalent of chewing gum and tape.

are not intended to be defined, at least not by science or logic; thus, we may as well let our feelings decide. The answer rests with our capacity to believe—and belief is based on confidence, but not certainty.

I believe evolution has shaped us to be a religious life form, which means that God has a voice inside us. By listening to that voice, many people find an extra source of strength, support, and meaning. Many people obtain a lot of help from God in this way. The capacity to sense the Divine is a gift, and those who have this ability possess a brilliant gem in their mind. God can help us because of the way evolution has shaped us. (See Appendix III: *Religion: The Role of the Genes,* p. 195.)

It is important to realize that even if the Divine is in us, it is not obvious that the world will be a better place as a consequence of our capacity to exercise free will. We are a product of the same process that shaped all other forms of life on Earth, and thus subject to the same limitations. We may see ourselves as a chosen species, but that does not make us infallible. It is not obvious that our conduct is going to save the environment—or ourselves. God may help us, but we need to help God.

Connecting with the Divine

The entity referred to as God has presumably been there all the time, but to our knowledge, it is only recently that a species has become able to sense it. The first human awareness may have occurred more than a million years ago, or perhaps only a hundred thousand years ago. At one point people began to imagine that there is a higher spirit permeating the world. Ever since we gained this capacity, the Divine presence has been a focus of life for many people.

During these years, mankind probably developed at least 100,000 belief systems. They all have stories, myths, and rituals. Most are long forgotten, but new ones are coming, so there are still a reasonable number of options to choose from. Every period and every culture in human history has its own description of God, and within each denomination there are several ways to worship. Actually, there appear to be as many ways to relate to God as there are people. It is up to each person to paint his or her personal portrait of God.[16]

Tribal people tend to regard the Divine as spirits inhabiting features of the nature surrounding them. Buddhism and Taoism can be seen as philosophical schools that worship their founders, but they also seem to aim at the same spirituality as the more typical religions. Some faiths, like Greek and Roman mythology, operate with a plethora of gods, while others see only a single Divine entity. It is interesting to note that even those who envision various deities with different functions typically consider them manifestations of a single, primary Divinity. The Hindus, for example, view Brahman as a shapeless phenomenon—a spirit that exists in both human and supernatural beings. They envision Brahman to be what the Universe is made of, a notion that is close to the present spiritual concept.

With so many portraits of God, it seems natural to ask whether all the alternatives really are versions of the same Divine principle? The present discussion is based on the answer being "yes," but the issue deserves elaboration.

Insight into human nature provides a reasonable starting point. Is our aptitude to sense God laid down in our genes, or is it just a cultural phenomenon that has arisen independently many times as a result of other aspects of the human psyche? If the first option is correct, our ability to feel the Force was formed by the process of evolution, and it follows that there must be a core common to all religions. If however, religion is a cultural phenomenon, it is less obvious that the different denominations have a shared core. A scientific assessment of human nature points toward the former alternative. (For a deeper discussion, see Appendix III: *Religion: The Role of the Genes,* p. 197.) In other words, it seems reasonable to envision a God that has bestowed upon us this capacity, by use of the evolutionary process, as a basis for making us aware of God. This implies that all denominations are reflections of the same Divine entity.[17]

It is reasonably obvious that there are a variety of ways to describe God. Differences in cultural and individual expression are

---

[16] To learn more about different creeds, I recommend A. F. C. Wallace, *Religion: An Anthropological View* (1966); or *Human Relations Area File* (available on a CD and from the Internet pages of Yale University).

[17] For discussions on whether the tendency to be religious is a consequence of evolution, see P. Boyer, *Religion Explained* (2002); S. Atran, *In God We*

even more evident in the field of fashion and music; yet for most people it is not a problem that, for example, choice of clothes or taste in tunes reflects personal preferences. Neither should it bother anyone that the way we relate to God reflects cultural and individual views.

It is the personal portraits people relate to. These are the ones that affect us. An obvious question is then whether some portraits, or rather the associated belief systems, are better than others. The question has nothing to do with how accurate these are. We do not have any correct answer to the question how God should be portrayed; thus, the question is solely about how the different creeds function.

There are many ways to build a relationship with another person; there are equally many ways to relate to God. Nevertheless, it is conceivable that some kinds of ties to fellow human beings—some forms of love and friendship—are more appropriate than others. The same may apply to our relationship with God.

———

Most religions are conservative, but even the most orthodox creeds change over time. They are able to adapt to new ideas without necessarily tearing down what was important in the original teachings. It should be possible to influence this direction of change—to help develop existing belief systems toward greater benefit for both religious adherents and mankind in general.

Science moves forward by generating ever more accurate and convincing descriptions of reality; when it comes to religion, however, it will never be a question of finding the one true description of the Divine. Instead, other issues do matter. For example, which denomination offers its congregation the most rewarding relationship with God, and which serves best the community it is a part of? We all have our strengths and weaknesses; the same may be said about belief systems. On the other hand, the intention should not be to end up with just one denomination. Each individual is unique, and we are part of, and influenced by, different cultural traditions. It is therefore an advantage to have a variety of creeds available so that as many as possible can find a place of worship that suits them.

———

Trust: The Evolutionary Landscape of Religion (2002); or B. Grinde, "The Biology of Religion: A Darwinian Gospel," *Journal of Social and Evolutionary Systems* 21 (1998): 19–28.

Nevertheless, it is possible to suggest some general recommendations.

A good creed helps us improve our capacity to sense God's presence. The objective of religious rituals and sermons should be to facilitate an engagement in the Divine, and thereby derive strength and joy from faith. That is, the icons and the narratives contained in the different belief systems are important because they provide nourishment for our emotions. In that way God may become a close friend and loving companion.

Each individual must find his or her own inner spiritual voice, but at the same time it is important to find a community for shared worship. Most people prefer to be a member of a denomination that caters to social connections and thereby directs followers toward building strong ties not only with God, but also with each other. Socializing is particularly important because religion has a lot to offer not just the individual, but also the community. Indeed, a central task for most denominations is to improve social life; for example, by encouraging compassion and by being involved in establishing useful codes of ethics.

It can be difficult to separate the spiritual from the material world. To avoid conflicts and unnecessary argument it may be preferable to have a belief system that accepts a scientific understanding of reality. Doctrines that are far removed from current rational thinking tend to be vulnerable to criticism and rejection. And if the congregation starts to doubt the anecdotes and accounts of their religion, they easily begin to doubt the existence of the underlying principle: They lose faith in God.

Moreover, in a world where all creeds are mixed together, it is important that the portraits of God do not annoy or counteract other ways of relating to the Divine. All religions should acknowledge that they are variations of a common theme. Accepting a scientific description of the Divine core ought to improve tolerance for alternative portraits. An additional advantage for those who see that all faiths revolve around the same Divine entity is that they can feel at home in any temple or church.

Early faiths were erected at a time when ways of living presumably were more uniform. In those days people rarely met with strangers raised under different cultural traditions. The world has changed. Present creeds may be advised to take into account that they are part of a vast, colorful, multicultural community, which means that they ought to be a little less assertive and a bit more open to variation than what was necessary ten thousand years ago.

At one point it was important to let devils and demons enter the doctrines for the purpose of scaring people away from evil actions. Today this may be less imperative. God may contribute toward making us more considerate and compassionate, but in this endeavor rewards may prove more useful than the fear of punishment. People prefer to be nice because it feels good, because their conscience tells them so, and because it is sensed as preferred by God, rather than because they otherwise risk Divine retaliation. In other words, the contribution religion may offer to improve human relations is presumably best served by a positive sentiment. Secular laws, which were not well developed a few thousand years ago, are today more suitable for handling punishment as a preventive agent. Notions such as purgatory and doomsday may be important in societies where secular regulatory systems are not functioning well, but of less use in developed countries.

In addition to the above suggestions, creeds should take into account that humans are shaped by the evolutionary process. It means that we are born with special qualities in the form of emotions and behavioral tendencies. Faith can adapt to these tendencies; that is, the various creeds can adjust to the inherent nature of being human, but at the same time discourage the less fortunate aspects of human nature. God and Man are intertwined. The better we understand our own species, the better we are able to find ways of relating to the Divine.

Most religions have evolved gradually over thousands of years. They may have their weaknesses, but they also bring along an ocean of wisdom. They have rituals that bring people together, both with each other and with God, and they provide support in difficult times. Moreover, faith provides a meaning of life, and a hope that everything is not over when the body eventually stops functioning. There may be room for improvements, but the wisdom inherited should not be wasted.

Prophets

Not only has Earth seen a considerable variety of creeds, there have also been numerous prophets. I use the term *prophet* for any person who helps others, either by kindness or by providing novel insight—where "others" may include family, community, or mankind. This implies that anyone can be a prophet. Yet, some people have had a greater and more profound impact compared to the average nice person. In virtue of their wisdom and their personal qualities they have meant a lot to a large number of people—not only their contemporaries, but generations to come. I shall mention a few of them, in chronological order: Abraham, Moses, Zarathustra, Confucius, Buddha, Plato, Aristotle, Jesus, Mohammed, Leonardo da Vinci, Nanak, Newton, Darwin, Baha'u'llah, and Einstein. Some initiated new religions, while others are famous primarily because they discovered significant pieces in our understanding of the Universe and life on Earth. For me they are all great prophets because they stood for appreciable contributions that have had wide-ranging ramifications.

Pioneers of a Unified Religion

Ten thousand years ago there may have been an even larger variety of religious legends than what we have today.[18] However, since neighboring tribes most likely would more or less follow the same doctrines, and since there was limited contact between distant tribes, this diversity would not be the cause of conflicts. Today there seem to be endless wars in which religious disparities play a central part. It is far from obvious that the differences in faith are the actual underlying cause of disputes, but spiritual sentiments are aroused. Religions are used, or misused, for the purpose of combat. In this situation, the world has a lot to gain by having prophets stand up and declare that everybody actually worship the same God, and that differences in doctrines do not matter.

---

[18] According to J. M. Diamond ("The Language Steamrollers," *Nature*, 389 [1997], p. 544–46), the main loss of linguistic diversity occurred between 3,000 and 10,000 years ago. The cause of the loss was presumably that agricultural societies and their cultures gained hegemony over a considerable part of the Earth. It seems likely that cultural diversity, including ways of worship, suffered a comparable loss.

King Asoka was one of the first persons known to see this point—and to make an attempt at dealing with the problem. Asoka lived from 304 B.C.–232 B.C. and is regarded as one of India's greatest leaders. He turned to Buddhism after witnessing the burden inflicted on the population by his own crusades, and from then on he worked for peace and consequently demanded equality and tolerance among religions. One of his decrees was: "It is forbidden to condemn other creeds—true believers honor whatever they have in them that is worth honoring."

Guru Nanak (1469–1539), the founder of Sikhism, was another Indian—with similar ideals. He managed to unite Muslims and Hinduists, rich and poor together, to worship under the same roof. Shortly thereafter yet another Indian turned up with a related mission: Akbar, a Mogul emperor (1542–1605), tried to create a synthesis of all creeds known to him. Again it was Hinduism and Islam that took center stage, as these were the dominant religions in the region at the time.

In the nineteenth century there were several prophets with visions of a common God. They all pointed out that the different stories of faith are simply variations on a common theme. The more famous ones include Sri Ramakrishna and his follower Vivekananda, as well as Baha'u'llah. Vivekananda expressed ideas related to those I try to promote: "The Divine exists on two levels—a higher level without any descriptive qualities, and a lower level of which the different creeds offer a depiction."

Sikhs, the Ramakrishna movement, and the Bahà'í faith are still with us today. So are related movements originating in the Jewish-Christian tradition, such as the Unitarian church.

Syncretism—the intermingling of religions based on the idea that they are all reflections of the same Divinity—is what the world needs more than ever. It is tempting to argue that anything else is heathen. Unfortunately, syncretism is difficult to achieve. Those who believe they have found the one and only true God are typically the ones who work hardest to gather souls for their particular version of faith, while those who realize that everyone worships the same deity do not have the same impetus to convert others. After all, in their minds the others are already conversant with the same God; consequently, it is difficult for the more open-minded congregations to grow big and strong.

Several of the prophets who are included in the history books realized that all belief systems are just variations of a common theme; for example, Akbar, Vivekananda, and Baha'u'llah. (See *Pioneers of a Unified Religion*, p. 56).

I hope that religions will eventually learn to deal with religiosity in a way that unites people rather than pitting people against each other.

————

It is interesting to note that those who probably had the greatest impact—both to their contemporaries and later generations—were not those who gave us the greatest leaps in understanding, but rather the prophets who taught us new ways of relating to the Divine. The supreme prophets, moreover, not only opened our eyes, but they were also living models inspiring a way of life. They managed to cultivate the best qualities of mankind: empathy, honesty, generosity, and responsibility. Even more striking, their effect on fellow humans was presumably not just a consequence of their teachings, but of an inner glow reflecting integrity, satisfaction, and peace of mind. *They taught us that by developing a relationship with God, it is possible to live with compassion and at the same time be happy.*

————

All the great prophets came up with novel notions, or at least they put together previous knowledge in new and constructive ways. They also managed to present their wisdom in a manner that appealed not only to those around them, but to people with different backgrounds; which is why their teachings live on. It is nevertheless important to keep in mind that the prophets acquired their wisdom from within a particular cultural tradition. Their prophecy reflects, and is limited by, both the cultural background and their personal characteristics. This implies that the details of what they put forth were not necessarily intended to stand as eternal truths. It also means that one may very well be critical of certain aspects of their teachings without showing lack of respect or diminishing their contributions.

Some devotees may perhaps disagree with the statement above, but I remain convinced that the prophets themselves would have agreed. For example, as Buddha supposedly said: "My words should be accepted only after careful consideration, not out of respect for me."

Unity with the Universe

It is possible to enter a state of mind where you have a particularly strong sensation of God's presence. Some people describe this as a feeling of "God's blessing" or "unity with the Universe." The condition apparently reflects a property that has been invested in us—perhaps for the purpose of having an awareness of the Divine. We know something about what parts of the brain are activated, and there are data suggesting that the feeling is associated with release of oxytocin, the "love hormone."[19]

The various descriptions of this state of mind typically include "a sense of unity." You perceive that you are part of the nature surrounding you, and rejoice in being a small brick in the vastness of the cosmos. Plants, animals, and people are all part of the fellowship. Stated another way, our ability to sense God's presence is at the same time a propensity to sense life *and* the Universe. Those who are capable of this experience describe it as a wonderful feeling. It is interesting to note that the fellowship recognized actually may reflect a more accurate way to understand reality compared to the everyday conception. The normal way of looking at life is to make a clear distinction between *me* and *everything else*. Evolution has equipped us with a strong tendency to distinguish our own person from the environment surrounding us. This dualistic point of view reflects the default setting of the mind, presumably because in evolutionary terms it is necessary that you promote the genes carried within you. When having a religious experience, it is possible to escape this dualism and instead feel united with your surroundings.

The point is that, physically speaking, it seems appropriate to describe the individual as "an integrated part of everything"—a brick with no obvious distinction from all the other bricks making up the Universe. You as a person, and thereby also your brain and mind, are made of the same elementary particles and atoms as the rest of the world. There is no definite distinction between the parti-

---

[19] Considerable research has been carried out for the purpose of understanding this state of mind. See, for example, A. Newberg, E. d'Aquili, and V. Rause, *Why God Won't Go Away* (2001); O. Blanke, S. Ortigue, T. Landis, and M. Seeck, "Stimulating Illusory Own Body Perceptions" *Nature*, 419 (2002): 269; or M. Beauregard and D. O'Leary, *The Spiritual Brain: A Neuroscientist's Case for the Existence of the Soul* (2007).

cles that comprise you and those outside your body; rather there is a flux of atoms going in and out. The skin forms a sort of boundary, but physically speaking this boundary is not that much more distinct than the transition between your liver and stomach, or between a rock and the surrounding soil. As seen from the outside, the entire Universe may be described as one big soup of elementary particles. A closer scrutiny reveals that the concentration varies enormously; in many places the particles have combined to form atoms and molecules, and in some locations the molecules are merged into larger units. But apart from these deviations, the Universe is a reasonably homogeneous soup. The building blocks, meaning the elementary particles, remain exactly the same throughout the vastness of space. You are in reality only a local accumulation.

I believe it may be useful to lean back occasionally and envision yourself as a part of a larger whole—a united cosmos—and allow this vision to mean something to you. The ability to feel an affinity with all living things, to sense a "unity with all," is not only pleasurable, but it may help us care for each other, and care for our corner of the Creation.

————

Both science and religion are important human endeavors. Science enables us to exploit the technological opportunities, whereas religion helps us with our emotional life and personal relations. We need both to cope with our role in the Theater of Earth. That is, we need to further expand our knowledge and to identify the best possible ways of relating to the Divine.

There are many problematic aspects of human nature. We are governed not only by love and compassion, but also by hatred, jealousy, and envy. God can help us to make the best of the situation. The more you let God inspire your life, the more joy and love the Divine offers you in return. Similarly, the better your local community provides for religion, the more benefits can be harvested from the positive forces therein—at least as long as the negative impact can be curtailed. When the beauty and complexity of the Universe becomes apparent, it is natural to perceive a Divine power. Science only describes the surface, the stage for all the miracles that make up the world; religion takes you to the core, to the script of the performance.

Reality may include more than what the traditional sciences are in a position to explain.

CHAPTER THREE

The arch from the Temple of Apollo on the island of Naxos, Greece.

The Creation

Creating a Narrative

According to the Christian Bible, God created the world a few thousand years ago and in the course of one week. As a first step He turned on the light, and then went on making the sea and the sky. On the sixth day He shaped man and used the seventh to rest and enjoy His work.

Non-believers tend to smile at this presentation. They know it cannot reflect reality: The Earth is a minor dot in a vast Universe that arose several billion years ago—and, of course, humans evolved from apes.

It is to be expected that science would gradually develop theories that differ from what is written in the Bible. After all, our understanding of the Universe has moved far beyond the knowledge available for those who shaped the Holy Scriptures. Thus, it is not the discrepancies that are interesting but the fact that people then were engaged with the same questions as we are today: *They tried to comprehend how the world came to exist, what life is all about, and whether there is any entity or force responsible for everything.*

Apparently mankind has always sought answers to these questions. Most creeds, from the imaginative stories of tribal people to intricate world religions, offer their version. It seems as if we have an internal drive aimed at understanding the cosmos and finding our roots. The ancient faiths presented their accounts; today we have a more detailed explanation but the task is the same. And as to some of the more fundamental questions, the answers for many of us are still the same: The Universe is the work of God; it exists for us, and we are a part of it.

We do not need to understand the origin of the Universe, or for that matter the foundation for our existence, in order to survive. Knowledge about distant galaxies and the evolution of life does not help us find food. Nevertheless, we are concerned; we *want* to find answers.

And answers we find. Many people feel that by learning about the Creation, they somehow move closer to the underlying Force; in that way they approach the phenomenon that has led to their very existence. Understandably, these people like to give the Force a name, and the one more commonly used is "God." I shall offer a reasonably detailed description of the current model of reality because I too believe it is important to know. I believe that insight brings us toward—not away from—God. Knowledge adds tiny brush strokes to our portrait of the Divine power, and thus provides a useful background for all doctrines of faith. The point was obvious for those alive 2,000 years ago, and it is still relevant today. Exploring the Creation requires, however, that one does not get entangled in the details of the old accounts.

I should mention that for those who are less interested, it is possible to read chapters four and five, which follow, without delving into this science-oriented chapter.

———

The discernible part of the Universe, i.e., that which we can observe, can induce a sense of humility and reverence. Perhaps that is why noticeable natural phenomena so often are part of what is worshiped. In many creeds the sun and the moon are considered Divine, while other creeds worship special trees, cliff formations, mountains, and rivers.

Science has given us insight into what these natural phenomena are actually about. Knowing that the sun is a burning ball of gas, like billions of other stars, may make it less mysterious. The same may be said when you realize that the sun only rises and falls because the Earth rotates around its own axis. But when you dig deeper into the machinery of the Universe, when you understand how unimaginably huge and complex it is, then the world regains all its mystery. And the phenomena you study, whether they are leaves on the trees or remote galaxies, stand out as fantastic and incredible. The invisible constituents, which only science can tell us about, present even more reasons to honor whatever power it was that shaped nature.

The task of understanding the Universe has been compared to solving a crossword puzzle where you happen to make a mistake at an early point. You manage to find words that seem to fit here and there, but many of them are actually wrong because they were chosen in order to fit with the first error. Sooner or later it stops. Parts of the crossword puzzle may be correct, but a complete solution appears to be beyond reach. Perhaps you manage to resolve a larger share of the puzzle, but you start to doubt whether any complete solution exists at all—whatever you try, there are always some issues that seem impossible to work out.

Our present solution to the riddles of the Universe is closer to reality than the explanations suggested by those who authored the Bible. You may laugh at their attempts, but two thousand years from now people will probably laugh at our fragile effort at filling in the answers. We describe bits and pieces of the Universe, but a complete understanding seems inaccessible. Perhaps it really is impossible to transform the workings of the Universe into man-made concepts; there may actually be factors that are forever beyond our capacity to comprehend. Then again, perhaps the one error we made early on was to insist on putting the word "science" in a spot where the correct answer demanded the word "Divinity."

Some scientists assume there are a vast number of universes.[1] Their reasoning is based on the fact that physical laws and the corresponding constants that rule our Universe have very peculiar qualities and values. Is it possible to imagine another universe set up with completely different physical laws, or, perhaps, with virtually the same laws as here, but with minor changes in the value of the constants? The answer is definitely "yes." There are at least 10^{500} options, but our version is exceptional. Our Universe is fantastic in that, among all these alternatives, it is probably the only one that could have given rise to us! Perhaps the only version that offers conditions for life to exist—at least life as we know it.

Consider, for example, the gravitational constant; it says something about the attraction between two celestial bodies. In our Universe it has the value $G=6.67428 \times 10^{-11}$ m^{3}kg^{-1}s^{-2}, and as previously mentioned this is the value that keeps our planet in its orbit around the sun.

Why does our Universe have these exact qualities? I see three possible explanations: The first is that there are many universes with

---

[1] A. Vilenkin, *Many Worlds in One: The Search for Other Universes* (2006); or M. Chown, "My Other World is a Porsche," *New Scientist* (October 7, 2006). For a deeper discussion on whether the existence of a "bio-friendly" universe is just a lucky fluke, see P. Davies, *The Goldilocks Enigma: Why Is the Universe Just Right for Life?* (2007).

different characteristics, but we are necessarily present in the one that offers an opportunity for life to develop. The second is that only this one Universe exists, and that we have been extremely lucky as to the shape of the physical laws. The third option is that a higher power stands behind these laws, a Divine Force that conceived and prepared the development toward what we experience today.

No one knows, and we may never have an answer. But the existence of a Divine power may be as likely an option as any other alternative.

It is tempting to take the above discussion one step further and ask whether the creation of the Universe could have been an intentional act?

For an atheist, it is difficult to envision that the design of the Universe would be governed by any purpose or plan, but not too long ago most people considered this as obvious. They felt that their existence could not be arbitrary; there *ought* to be a reason why humankind appeared on Earth. The authors of the Bible tried to convey this message; but as the sciences dug deeper into reality many people lost their faith in a creative Force with Providence.

The strange thing is that when science enthusiasts, including myself, feel that we are approaching a complete description of the Universe, one that precludes any room for Divine entities, then, in some respect, we are actually close to where the early religious accounts started. The point being that the deeper we dig into the processes that have led to our existence, the more signs of premeditation we find. The present scientific narrative is full of strange phenomena and surprising twists, which make it difficult to perceive that the result is due solely to chance. This chapter describes some of them.

We are alive. We are solid evidence of our own existence. One may argue that if the Universe had been different, humans would not exist, and consequently no one would be around to either ask or answer inscrutable questions. On the other hand, even those who consider the world to be no more than the result of an almost infinite number of improbable events still lack answers as to how and why it all got started.

The best response to the question of intentionality is probably that it depends on what content one chooses to include in this word.

The terms we use to express ideas about intentions, or about the meaning of life, are created for the purpose of exploring the human mind, not Divine power. Even if one accepts that all the weird things that have happened, and that have led to our existence, can hardly be ascribed to sheer coincidence, it is not obvious that the word "intention" gives rise to the appropriate associations. The underlying Force of the Universe may include some sort of impetus, but hardly any human consciousness, and thus no intention in the normal sense of the word. Yet, when we describe the Universe, or the postulated Divine Force entailed therein, our account is necessarily confined to the options available in human language. It is important to keep that in mind when reading the narrative of the Creation.

The Birth of a Universe

Going back a few decades, many scientists assumed that the Universe has always been here, that there was no beginning; today, however, the dominating thought is that it started with a phenomenon referred to as the Big Bang. We are pretty sure that this event happened approximately 13.7 billion years ago.[2]

The Big Bang theory presumes that right at the start there was an entity referred to as a *singularity*—that is, a single point without extension and with matter condensed in a state of infinitely high temperature and pressure. In fact, the theory implies that the entire Universe was assembled in this one spot.

Does this sound like a rational idea?

On the face of it, the present scientific version of reality appears less convincing than the Book of Genesis. The problem is partly due to the absurdity of the concept of a singularity, and that we know next to nothing about what it really is. Our laws of physics cannot explain this condition. Even our imagination finds it hard to conjure an image of such an object. In fact, we do not know the true nature of the starting point for our Universe, and we have even fewer clues as to how this starting point came to exist, or why the singu-

---

[2] For a more precise account of the Big Bang, consider for example C. H. Lineweaver and T. M. Davis, "Misconceptions About the Big Bang," *Scientific American* (March 2005): 24–33; and M. S. Turner, "The Origin of the Universe," *Scientific American* (September 2009): 22–29.

A gate on the island of Santorini, Greece. It leads toward the ancient
city of Akrotiri, which may have been the legendary Atlantis.

larity suddenly began to expand. Nevertheless, the Big Bang theory
is the best model we now have for how it all started.

According to the Bible, in the beginning there was God. The
concept of singularity can be interpreted as an attempt to give God
a scientific name. Both the word singularity and the word "God"
describe the origin of the Universe; our language and our capacity
to comprehend are equally inappropriate when it comes to specify
whichever of the two words one prefers to apply.

We can, however, say something about what happened next.

—————

The Universe began with expansion, and it has continued to expand ever since. The Big Bang does not imply that substances contained in the singularity were thrown out as in an explosion; instead
matter moved apart due to an abrupt and incessant enlargement of
the space that the Universe occupies. The Universe grows bigger
every day. During the very first moment when the Universe came

into being, the expansion was extremely fast due to a special process we refer to as "inflation." That is to say, the Universe was "blown up" from a point without extension to a dawning world within a fraction of a second. In fact, this initial expansion presumably even broke the cosmic speed limit, i.e., the speed of light.

The main problem with regard to producing theories for the event concerns this first, brief moment of time. After only a tiny fraction of a second, we do have a theory.[3] That does not mean we *know* what happened, but at least we can fashion models that *seem credible* based on current knowledge. According to inflation theory, the Universe had then grown to an embryo a few kilometers in diameter.

The idea that everything has a common origin explains a phenomenon that is not as obvious as it may seem: No matter in which direction of the heavenly realms you look, or rather direct your telescope, what you see is more or less the same. If you glance beyond our own galaxy, the Milky Way, you will find other galaxies, spread out in all possible directions and distances from Earth. Moreover, the building blocks—that is, the elementary particles—are similar everywhere, in stark contrast to snowflakes. The Universe is, in other words, "homogenous." Matter is not evenly distributed on a smaller scale; it is clustered in galaxies, stars, and other celestial bodies, but on a sufficiently large scale things are rather uniform.

The Universe did not have to be the same all over. If, for example, our planet had been close to the edge, then we should have observed more galaxies in the direction toward the center. Furthermore, if it had not all been created in the same instant, then some parts of the universe might have been constructed with other types of elementary particles compared to those making up our galaxy; or at the least with differing prevalence of the various particles and atoms. Which is not the case. If you cut out any larger chunk of the Universe. you will find that it contains pretty much the same sort of atoms and particles. The same holds for the physical processes: What we observe in our corner of the Universe presumably happens all over. The one possible exception being the process of evolution.

---

[3] The time point 10^{-32} second has been suggested. See M. Riordan and W. A. Zajc, "The First Few Microseconds," *Scientific American* (May 2006): 24–31.

At the end of the first, brief inflation period, the Universe was still terribly hot—at least 10^{30} °C, so hot that all substances were torn apart to their smallest units: the elementary particles. Even the particles that until recently were considered to be nature's smallest units—namely protons, neutrons, and mesons—did not exist. Reality was instead made up of smaller fragments, such as quarks, leptons, and gluons. These are the actual elementary particles according to our present knowledge of physics. Together they formed a kind of gooey, super-hot porridge.[4]

Gradually the temperature decreased while the porridge continued to expand. After about 10^{-6} seconds, the elementary particles began to fuse together to form protons and neutrons (each consisting of three quarks held together by gluons), but it took a few seconds before the protons and neutrons had calmed down sufficiently to gather in atomic nuclei. In the beginning there were only the nuclei corresponding to the smallest atoms: hydrogen, deuterium (an isotope of hydrogen), and helium.

What we may consider the birth of our Universe was completed in a fraction of the time required for a human to be born. The first few seconds saw the atomic nuclei and other particles being spread out over a huge area, while the temperature dropped to levels we can begin to comprehend. This process has in fact never stopped; concomitant with the expansion we see a continuous decrease in average temperature.

One of the strange things that we do not quite understand is why the soup of particles, even from an early point on, became inhomogeneous. In some areas matter became denser than in other places. Consequently, the soup gradually turned into a giant sponge-like structure, where certain regions were more or less devoid of substance. We assume that the starting point was a uniform singularity that spread evenly in all directions. So why did the soup not retain the same density everywhere? The cosmologists like to blame *quantum fluctuations,* which is just a fancy way of saying random variations. Some scientists might suggest that a more honest answer would be to admit our ignorance.

What we do know is that, due to the force of gravity, these irregularities became more noticeable as time went by. In other words, matter gradually accumulated in celestial objects. The devel-

---

[4] A. Gefter, "Liquid Universe," *New Scientist* (October 16, 2004): 35–37.

opment of irregularities was a somewhat unexpected twist, but it was an essential factor in creating a universe with stars and planets—and thus a universe with the facilities required to give rise to humans.[5]

As we shall see, there have been many such seemingly unpredictable occurrences in the history of the Universe—surprising events that have been necessary in order to provide suitable conditions for life to evolve. We may postulate some sort of explanation, or we may regard the events as flukes; but there is also the choice of considering them to be signs of a supreme God.

Part of the problem with describing the first fractions of a second is that the physical laws, as we know them from the present Universe, became active only after the first round of supernatural expansion. According to the *Grand Unified Theory,* or a version of it anyway, there was nevertheless one governing physical force right from the beginning.[6] After the first expansion phase, the one universal force postulated by this theory was divided among four players—namely, the basic forces that we know today: electromagnetic force, weak nuclear force, strong nuclear force, and gravity. Today these four basic forces have very different properties, but when they were united as a single power, they were presumably equally strong. The most problematic part of this model has been to incorporate gravity along with the other three. Oddly, gravity is the only one of these forces that everybody can relate to—after all, it is what keeps your feet on the ground, yet it is the one we understand the least.

These four players control everything we observe. They rule the world by determining the interaction between the various elementary particles (at the microscopic level), and celestial bodies (on the macroscopic level). The physical constants are telling us something about the strength of these forces, and thus define the rules of interactions.

It took some 380,000 years for more tangible things to happen. The average temperature of the universe had fallen to around

---

[5] Thus random fluctuations are ultimately responsible for our solar system. See M. S. Turner, "Quarks and the Cosmos," *Science* 315 (2007): 59–61.

[6] See, for example, M. Kaku, *Parallel Worlds: The Science of Alternative Universes and Our Future in the Cosmos* (2004).

2,700 °C, and the Universe had grown to a considerable size. At this point, atoms such as hydrogen and helium were formed. True atoms consist of both atomic nuclei and electrons orbiting these, but earlier on the temperature was too high for the electrons to settle down.

The formation of atoms had an interesting consequence. Prior to their existence, the photons, which are responsible for visible light, could not move freely. They existed for brief moments only, soon to be absorbed by interactions with other particles. The establishment of atoms caused the "liberation" of photons. From then on they could live forever; in fact, many of the photons that existed at that time are still roaming around in the Universe at the speed of light. We refer to these photons as the *cosmic microwave background radiation*. (The significance of these microwaves is revealed in *The Age and Size of the Universe*, below.)

The Age and Size of the Universe

Photons are the unit of electromagnetic radiation. The properties of these rays depend on the wave length. Those between 400 and 720 nm constitute visible light, while photons with longer wave lengths (from 1 mm to 100 km) are called radio waves in that they are used for broadcasting radio and TV. A part of the radio-wave spectrum is referred to as microwaves, which includes the radiation used by your microwave oven.

In the first time period the Universe was too hot for photons to survive; however, when the Universe was still a mere baby of 380,000 years it had cooled down sufficiently to allow the photons to move around. This was good news for the photons, as well as for those of us who want to understand how the Universe came about, because there are still photons left from this "first dawn," and they tell us a story.

The ancient photons have gradually lost much of their energy and concomitantly changed to longer wave lengths. Today they are referred to as the *cosmic microwave background radiation* and have wave lengths similar to the microwaves used in broadcasting—which is how they were discovered since they cause interference in the form of noise on the radio. In fact, you may still "see" them on TV. Some of the flicker on the screen, which occurs when the receiver cannot find any program, is due to photons dating back to the early Universe.[7]

With the help of satellites, scientists have been able to take "photos" of these photons. A careful analysis of the photos yields a sort of portrait of the baby Universe. In fact, the microwave background helps us estimate its present age: Some 13.7 billion years have passed since the Big Bang.

The size of the Universe is a bit more difficult. The part that we can see is no problem: In whatever direction you point a telescope, the farthest galaxies are about 13 billion light years away. Thus the *observable Universe* is a sphere with a radius of 13 billion light years. The problem is that any objects farther away than 13.7 billion light years are necessarily invisible simply because the light emitted from these objects has not had the time to reach Earth.

It seems unlikely that the Earth is at the exact center of the Universe; thus, the observable galaxies presumably reflect only a fraction of it all. Based on other evidence, some scientists have suggested that the real radius may be 46 billion light years, which corresponds to 10^{27} m. The actual size of our Universe would then be 4×10^{32} cubic light years, or roughly 3×10^{80} cubic meters. Large enough to feel small.

Planets, Stars, and Galaxies

For a considerable period of time not much happened except for the ongoing expansion and cooling. Matter gradually gathered into vast "clouds," but it probably took a billion years before the density became sufficient for the clouds to form stars. Several stars typically appeared in the same area; thus, they would group together in what we call galaxies. Galaxies gathered in galaxy clusters, or they fused together to form larger galaxies.

There is more above heaven and Earth than you might imagine. The deeper one gazes into space, the more surprises and greater complexity become visible. For example, we still find large clouds of particles, which we refer to as *nebulae*. They are either remnants of exploding stars, or simply congregations of particles that have yet to

---

[7] P. J. E. Peebles, *Principles of Physical Cosmology* (1993).

develop into stars. Some are large enough to form entire galaxies, and we do not know why they have not done just that. In other places we observe what we assume to be baby galaxies, enormous accumulation of matter within a single object. They are called quasars and send out more energy than any other celestial object. A single quasar can give as much light as one thousand billion suns. Unfortunately they are only visible with telescopes; even the nearest ones are very far away.

The Universe certainly started out in a dramatic fashion, but one might perhaps have thought that after 13.7 billion years things should have calmed down. The rowdiness of youth may be over; the first 6 billion years saw a cosmic firework of star births and colliding galaxies.[8] The present Universe is more peaceful, but the show is not at the end; strange things are still happening. Stars are not stable units, they are born, grow old, and die, which is fortunate for us, because otherwise we would not have experienced life and death on Earth.

Stars consist of an enormous cluster of atomic nuclei in a kind of a gas phase referred to as plasma. This means that there is no fixed point in a star. On the other hand, the nuclei are packed considerably closer together than the typical gases we experience here on Earth; the pressure is high and the temperature can reach several million degrees Celsius. The energy that maintains this temperature and causes the stars to emit light stems from nuclear reactions. In young stars it is primarily a question of hydrogen nuclei merging to form helium nuclei; in older stars the helium nuclei fuse together to form a variety of larger elements. The energy from these reactions radiates outwards and helps prevent the gravitational force from pulling the nuclei even closer together.

Einstein has taught us that mass and energy are really just two manifestations of the same thing. This implies that mass can be converted to energy—and vice versa—in processes governed by the equation $E = mc^2$, where E stands for energy, m for mass, and c is the speed of light. As light travels rather fast (300,000 km/s), there is a lot of energy packed into even a tiny amount of matter. In nuclear reactions, a fraction of the mass of the nuclei involved is transformed into energy.

---

[8] A. J. Barger, "The Midlife Crisis of the Cosmos," *Scientific American* (January 2005).

Pagodas near the Cape of Laotieshan, China.

No star lasts forever. At some point all the fuel is spent, and when that happens the star is "dead" in that it will no longer emit light. Interestingly, the giant stars die first, while the smaller ones last considerably longer. This is because the bigger they are, the more intense are the nuclear reactions, and consequently the faster they use up their fuel—some in no more than a million years. Our own sun is a rather ordinary star, and will probably live for 10 billion years. After barely 5 billion years, it is still in its prime.

Stars are not just of different sizes, they also have different properties. When a large star dies, there are two options as to what can happen: either it collapses or the whole thing explodes. In the former case, all the matter that constitutes the star is pulled together in a process that may not stop until everything is crammed together and the nuclei split up into elementary particles. The star has turned into a state of infinite density and temperature—that is, a state akin to what the Universe was like at the moment everything began! A state that is consequently given the same name—a singularity.

The object so formed is called a *black hole*. Black because it is so dense that the gravitational force keeps even photons from slipping out. Human vision depends on light, which is made up of photons; consequently, no one will ever be able to see a black hole. We can, however, observe its effect on the surroundings and thereby find out where they are located.

An interesting point regarding black holes is that they stand for what may be considered "cosmic censorship": They remain outside the human capacity to explore, other than with superficial and indirect methods. It is as if the Universe should have at least one mysterious entity that is more or less outside human intellectual competence. Coincidentally, this entity is akin to the original state of the Universe.

Most galaxies seem to have a black hole in their center. The enormous gravitational force created by the singularity causes material to be sucked in from the surrounding area. Consequently, black holes are expanding; in fact, sooner or later everything, including our planet, may end up inside one of them. It is hard to imagine anything closer to an Armageddon. If you plunge into a black hole head first, the difference in gravitational force from head to feet will cause your body to be elongated to the shape of spaghetti. Fortunately, there is no reason to worry; nothing suggests that you will experience "spaghettification" in the near future; certainly not during the next billion years.

Scientists like to point out that what happened once can happen again. If the Universe originated from a singularity, then a new universe may emerge from the singularities we call black holes. In fact, the black holes may be a sort of "recycling device": Eventually all matter is brought back to a single singularity, which means the time is ripe for the creation of a new universe.

Some cosmologists go one step further and argue that if the preconditions for creating a universe rest with the production of certain physical conditions—namely, those that describe a singularity— then we humans should be able to create our very own "universe." Pretty ambitious, but not necessarily impossible. Briefly, the task involves the compression of a sufficient amount of matter into an extremely small volume with the help of a particle accelerator. In theory, the matter should eventually collapse into the condition referred to as a singularity. The question then is whether there is anything present that can turn on the inflation process, the extremely rapid expansion denoting the start of a new universe. It certainly would be an exciting experiment to follow, but it may require a bit of patience. Expect to wait a few billion years for anything to happen. And, of course, part of the thrill is to find out whether you are to be a part of the singularity.

It says in the Bible that God created man in His *own* image. Does that mean we were created to be gods? Will we at some point develop the powers of God? Apparently we do not shy away from trying, in that we attempt to exploit all the possibilities offered by the laws of the Universe. We are, for example, able to produce certain types of nuclear reactions, the main energy source of the Universe. We can re-create, but to a limited extent control, perhaps the most important process that takes place—namely the fusion of hydrogen nuclei. As pointed out, most of the energy the sun produces stems from the fusion of hydrogen, and our hydrogen bombs are based on the same process. Moreover, we have gained the competence required to direct the process of evolution. But should we really try to create a universe out of particle porridge? It may prove to be a rather hot porridge. Before we feel called upon to control a universe, we should perhaps show that we are able to manage a planet.

For a star, the alternative to collapse is even more dramatic. Nothing compares to the display of an exploding giant star; the event is referred to as a *supernova*. Supernovas liven up the Universe in two ways: They constitute the most spectacular events in space, and they dish out a product required for life to evolve on planets.

Hydrogen fusion bombs are several thousand times more powerful than the traditional fission-based atomic bomb dropped over Hiroshima. Fission implies that atomic nuclei (for example, those of uranium) are split up. Our man-made bombs are still no more than farts compared to what the sun produces of energy every second. The sun, however, is next to nothing compared to a supernova. An exploding star can send out more energy in one instant than the sun does throughout its entire ten billion years of life.

The most important difference between human nukes and the process that takes place in the sun is that, while the nuclear bombs burn off all their fuel in an instant, in the sun the nuclear reactions are harnessed, which is obviously good news. Supernovas are more like a nuclear bomb. We do not quite understand why some stars explode while others burn gently and slowly like a candle. Actually, the more surprising observation is that the nuclear reactions taking place in our sun do not run wild. The explanation seems to rest with minor deviations in the composition of stars, and a delicate balance of the strength of the basic forces of the Universe.

The interesting and striking point is that life on Earth depends on this balance. As we shall see, life requires not only stable stars, but also the occasional explosion.

———

The hydrogen atom is the smallest of the more than 100 different elements known to man. Yet, if we measure the combined mass of all the atoms present in the Universe, hydrogen comprises some 74%. Moreover, hydrogen is the starting point for the formation of other elements. In order to form larger atoms, nuclear reactions are required, which is what happens inside the stars. The primary product is helium, the second smallest element, which makes up 24% of the Universe. Only in the later stages of their lives do the stars begin to produce more heavy atoms. For some vaguely understood reason their preferred products include oxygen, carbon, and nitrogen. Coincidentally, life is based on these exact elements: hydrogen, carbon, oxygen, and nitrogen. Together they have the chemical properties required to perform miracles—in the form of living organisms. We know pretty well the chemical properties of all the various elements, and it appears that other combinations most likely would not do the trick. Thus, there are reasons to thank the stars for their effort: Your presence depends on it. Yet, it is a mystery why stars focus their nuclear reactions toward the production of the exact atoms suitable for life.

Due to the high temperature, life inside a star is out of the question. Living organisms depend on molecules, which is what you get when atoms bond to each other, but molecules cannot form inside stars. What makes the supernovas so important is that the explosion disperses into the space beyond the various atoms that are formed. Sooner or later the atoms may again condense to form celestial bodies, and some of them end up in cooler and more solid structures, such as our planet.

This is presumably what happened 4.6 billion years ago. A supernova explosion took place near by. An enormous collection of atoms was blown out, and those that went in a certain direction happened to hit an existing cloud of particles. Together, the material from the two entities, the supernova and the cloud, formed a colossal disc, which was flattened by the impact of the collision. Due to the increase in density, the disc contracted. The cloud was presumably rotating even before it was hit, but the rate of rotation increased as matter was pulled together, in such a way as you would pull in your legs and arms during a somersault. This spinning disc was the start of our solar system. The density within the disc allowed for most of the matter to assemble eventually into various celestial bodies.

In its central part the concentration of particles was particularly high. The pressure and temperature rose, the latter to more than a million degrees Celsius. In other words, the conditions were suitable for the initiation of nuclear reactions, and thus the birth of a star. We got our sun. Farther out, the matter gathered in either small solid bodies or in dense gas clouds. Some of these objects gradually increased in size as they collided and fused with each other. A few of them reached the size of planets; others remained small and are today comets and asteroids. Together they make up our solar system, our home, a small corner of the galaxy, which again is an insignificant speck in the vastness of the Universe.[9]

––––––

Our planet was born in an inferno of collisions. At one point a particularly large object, probably a small planet the size of Mars hit the Earth. Rather than fusing to become one, the impact caused a big chip to be torn out. The object so formed ended up circling the Earth. We got a moon.

The smallest objects orbiting the sun are referred to as meteoroids. They may range in size from a grain of sand to a boulder. There are still a considerable number of meteoroids out there; and on a clear night those hitting the Earth's atmosphere create streaks

––––––

[9] There is still a lot we do not know about how the Earth came to exist. For a more detailed discussion, I suggest H. Muir, "Earth Was a Freak," *New Scientist* (March 29, 2003): 24; or D. J. Stevenson, "A Planetary Perspective on the Deep Earth," *Nature* 451 (2008): 261–65.

of light that we call shooting stars. The light is due to the heat created by the friction air exerts on these high-speed rocks. Most of them simply evaporate due to the heat while still in the atmosphere, but a few are sufficiently large so that the remnants hit the ground.

Comets are larger than typical meteoroids and asteroids and are made mainly of ice combined with clumps of dust or rock. Being struck by a comet is a rather unpleasant experience, but luckily there are relatively few comets left so they are unlikely to hit us. On the other hand, as will be discussed in the next section, *Life on Earth,* if it had not been for at least one such collision, at an appropriate point of time in relation to the evolution of life, we would probably not be here.

———

Everything is in motion. Nothing stays where it was. You may be resting in your chair while reading this, but that does not mean you are stationary: The Earth rotates around its own axis while at the same time orbiting the sun. The latter movement has a speed of about 30 km/s; still it takes a year for a complete loop. The whole solar system travels in relation to other stars in our Milky Way Galaxy, and the entire galaxy spins around its central part. Even with a speed of 217 km/s, our solar system needs 250 million years to circle once around our galaxy. And what about the galaxy: Does it still move away from where it all began?

Movement may not be the right word here. The Universe expands so that the galaxies end up farther away from each other, but in a way this is a question of an expansion of space, rather than movement of the various bodies enwrapped in space. The situation is somewhat like a muffin with raisins. As you bake the muffin, the raisins will drift apart due to the swelling of the cake.

———

We have seen that the Universe has a richer variety of players—everything from quarks to quasars—than what even the most imaginative mythological story has ever invented. The list of known elementary particles is getting longer. The same goes for the list of secondary particles and atoms formed as well as the types of molecules the atoms combine into. As for the larger entities of the Universe, there are still objects and phenomena that we have only just begun to understand. The Universe is an extremely complex affair, and that statement holds true even without taking living organisms into account.

My description has so far only touched a minor part of what constitutes the world. The strange thing is that the matter described above (elementary particles, atoms, and molecules), which we are starting to get a grip on, apparently makes up only some 4% of the Universe. We hardly know anything about the remaining 96%; barely enough to assume that there has to be something else, something even weirder, out there. Recent scientific discoveries have forced us to postulate the existence of forms of energy, or esoteric substances, beyond what the known elementary particles are up to. Thus the stars, which were previously assumed to constitute the majority of matter, actually only represent one-fourth of regular matter, which implies only one percent of the total. The remaining regular matter is present as free-floating atoms, or atoms gathered in planets or enormous clouds that do not emit light.

Two postulated types of substances presumably make up the larger part of the Universe. One is referred to as *dark matter,* which stands for 22% of the total; the other we call *dark energy.* The latter is the bigger player, comprising 74% of the total. We know next to nothing as to what these two terms actually reflect, but some scientists envision novel elementary particles with qualities very different from the particles that have been described so far.[10]

Actually these two entities are not much more than names for our ignorance. Astrophysicists are simply incapable of explaining certain phenomena, and the option chosen is to postulate dark matter and dark energy. For the religiously minded, the underlying phenomena can very well be seen as reflections of a Divine force. (The text *Dark Forces,* below, delves a little bit deeper into the mystery.)

Dark Forces

The reason why scientists postulated the existence of dark matter and dark energy was that certain observations became impossible to explain without filling up the Universe with a lot more than just the observable collection of atoms and elementary parti-

---

[10] See for example, J. Hogan, "Unseen Universe: Welcome to the Dark Side," *Nature* 448 (2007): 240–45; or M. S. Turner, "Quarks and the Cosmos," *Science* 315 (2007): 59–61.

cles. The relevant observations are primarily associated with the movement of celestial objects and the expansion of the Universe. The amount of dark matter and dark energy was calculated based on the impact they must have in order to make the data fit with the preferred model of reality.[11]

The reason why we know next to nothing about the darker components is that they hardly interact with regular matter. Humans are composed of atoms, and our senses and scientific instruments are designed to register that sort of matter. Consequently, it has proven particularly difficult to find out anything about these mysterious "other" components. The term "dark" does not imply dark forces in the shape of malignant monsters, but simply "dark" in the sense of invisible to eyes and instruments.

On the other hand, if dark matter and energy had absolutely no interaction with regular substances, there would be no reason to postulate their existence. Thus both have a distinct way of manifesting themselves: Dark matter is a sort of gravitational force, and is included in the model of reality because normal gravity is too weak to explain certain observations, such as why the stars of a spinning galaxy do not leave the galaxy due to the centrifugal force. In other words, dark matter helps keep celestial units together. It appears to have about the same distribution in the Universe as do atoms and elementary particles.[12]

Dark energy is even more obscure. Its postulation was a response to a rather bewildering observation made quite recently. According to Big Bang theory, the Universe started by having everything move apart at an enormous speed, but then the gravitational force kicked in and gradually reduced the velocity. So far so good, but the strange thing is that five billion years ago the situation apparently changed. The galaxies started to move apart at an increasing speed. In order to explain this, the cosmologists filled the Universe with an evenly distributed dose of dark energy. The only presumed attribute of dark energy is to act as repellant pushing celestial objects apart.[13] Fortunately, the gravitational and anti-gravita-

---

[11] Actually some scientists try to find alternative explanations for these observations. See T. Clifton and P. G. Ferreira, "Does Dark Energy Really Exist?" *Scientific American* (April 2009): 32–39.

[12] H. Muir, "The Cosmic Controller," *New Scientist* (June 17, 2006): 47–49.

[13] S. Battersby, "Dark Energy," *New Scientist* (April 5, 2003): 30–33.

tional forces of the Universe seem to be balanced to the extent required for the formation of stars and planets.[14]

Our ancestors added novel gods or heavenly forces when they saw something they could not explain. The ancient Norse God Thor, for example, creates thunder. Scientists do not appreciate that strategy; they prefer to postulate new particles or heavenly forces. Perhaps the difference is not that drastic.

It is indeed a peculiar Universe in which we live—strange that it exists at all, strange that it would originate apparently out of nowhere, and strange that it is not just a boring soup of particles dispersed over the eternity of space but instead a teeming theater where nothing stands still and the most incredible things happen. In fact, as seen from Earth, the Universe is an enormous, chaotic drama. Yet there seems to be a plan; you get the sense that the plot is developing in the direction of something ever more grand and impressive. I cannot imagine a more exciting performance. It is not necessary to postulate any spiritual Force in order to describe this drama; yet, it is rather tempting to include such an entity. It is tempting to assume the presence of an underlying Force quite different from anything science can even begin to describe. The deeper you delve into the workings of the Universe, the stronger are the sensations that something stands behind it all. The theater appears to have a director.

Life on Earth

There is one phenomenon that seems as incredible as the creation of the Universe: the evolution of life.

We humans are surrounded by living organisms. Wherever we go there are plants, animals, and humans—or at the very least bacterial life forms. Life seems so obvious because, after all, we ourselves are an example. But if we look more carefully at what is actually required for life to exist and operate at the complexity we see today, a planet covered with living organisms is not that obvious at all. When we learn about the extreme intricacy required to manage

[14] C. J. Conselice, "The Universe's Invisible Hand," *Scientific American* (February 2007): 24–31.

even the tiniest cell, and the balanced interactions of billions of cells in millions of species, our organic world seems more and more like a giant wonder. Our presence is more like . . . "a miracle."

The point is that, whether we gaze at stars or at trees in the forest, our eyes only glimpse the surface. Beneath this façade it is hardly possible to imagine the complexity of the world. Consider our own bodies. An enormous number of components and carefully adjusted processes are required to make just one of the cells function. To have a life, a highly coordinated collaboration is required—among some hundred billion cells.

The Universe would have survived without any forms of life, as it most likely did for several billion years. The fact that organisms exist is in a way the crowning glory of our Universe. To have a species with the capability to understand what it is all about is an even more astonishing achievement. *We* are a bigger sensation than any of the stories told in the Bible.

Living organisms are indeed a strange phenomenon. In fact, we have problems defining exactly what life is; sometimes it is difficult to distinguish between the living and the dead. (See *Dead or Alive,* below, for a discussion.)

Dead or Alive

It is difficult to distinguish between the living and the dead. Consider, for example, the questions: When does a new human being become alive? And at what point is it correct to state that life has ended? We need suitable definitions, but they are not obvious; consequently, doctors, lawyers, and philosophers have fought over these issues for centuries. Then consider a person who is kept alive solely by hospital devices, but without any apparent brain activity. Should that person be buried? What if the doctors at some point learn how to restart the brain? Even in the absence of a particular intervention, there are cases where consciousness was absent for years and then slowly re-emerged. Thus, even when the person is kept alive in what appears to be a vegetative state, without detectable brain activity, it is difficult to decide at what point to give up.

The situation is not easy even at the beginning of life. At what point is an embryo alive? Some would say at conception, while others will argue that up to three months it is fair to terminate the pregnancy without considering it murder. Others might argue "at first breath."

It becomes even more difficult to distinguish between dead or alive when moving beyond human beings. What about a seed? It can be several thousand years old before it suddenly begins to sprout because it finally ends up in the right spot. Then again, most seeds lose their ability to grow within a few years, so how do we know if a seed is a living entity? And are viruses alive? They are everywhere. There are a lot more of them than all other organisms combined, both in terms of types and number. They are, in a way, the Earth's biggest success story, yet on their own they are dead as stone; only when they reach the inside of a suitable cell will they start to reproduce and thus take on some of the characteristics of an organism. Common definitions of life emphasize qualities such as capacity of self-maintenance, propagation, and adaptation through evolution.[15] Though there is some doubt about viruses, they do join the living on the basis of these criteria.

In the laboratory we can produce viral genetic material that, if delivered to a suitable cell, will prove to be alive. Does that mean we are able to create life?[16]

The problem with distinguishing between the living and the dead is not to be blamed on biological design, but is rather a consequence of the human desire for clear definitions and unambiguous categories. To describe what life is about, one runs into a semantic dilemma not unlike the problem of defining God. Nature is not designed to yield tidy definitions based on the haphazard nature of human language. Reality is too complex. So whether God is alive—well, that is up to you.

Some 98% of the atoms in the Universe are either hydrogen or helium. Oxygen and carbon are number three and four on the list of common elements, while nitrogen comes in at seventh place, after neon and iron. Of these elements, hydrogen, helium, and neon are volatile gases, but oxygen and nitrogen also occur in gaseous form at the temperatures we are accustomed to. Gas is an inappropriate building material for a planet that you can walk on; however, if ele-

[15] R. Hazen, "What Is Life?" *New Scientist* (November 18, 2006): 46–51.
[16] B. Holmes, "What Do You Need to Create Life?" *New Scientist* (February 12, 2005): 29–33.

ments bond to each other to form molecules or salts, they can create something more tangible—rocks for example. Helium and neon are incapable of forming that kind of relationship; consequently, there is not much left of them on Earth; on the other hand, hydrogen, oxygen, carbon, and nitrogen readily combine with each other, as well as with other elements, which salvaged their presence on our planet.

The composition of Earth is neither representative of the distribution of elements in the Universe, nor of the composition of the gas cloud from which our solar system was formed. The atoms of the four inner planets (Mercury, Venus, Earth, and Mars) are selected for their capacity to form solid matter. The larger planets beyond, such as Jupiter and Saturn, are composed primarily of gas.

The most common elements on Earth are: iron (32%), oxygen (30%), silicon (15%), magnesium (14%), and sulfur (3%). At an early point there was a reallocation of elements between the inner and outer part of the globe. The surface crust is only a thin shell (10km to 50km thick) which consists largely of rocks based on oxygen compounds such as silica oxide and aluminum oxide. The interior is mostly iron. Below the crust, the temperature is high—up to 7,000 °C; therefore, both the iron in the core and the magma of the mantle between the core and the surface are in a liquid state.

At first glance our planet may not appear that special, but it is. When compared with other planets in our solar system, several key features are certainly unique, but the particular constellation of properties is most likely highly unusual for planets anywhere in the Universe. A number of these features are indeed required for the planet to support life, as well as for directing the evolutionary process toward complex organisms.

One such feature is simply Earth's size. If the Earth had been smaller or larger it would most likely not have the core of fluid iron required to set up a magnetic field. Besides being a useful feature for anyone appreciating the use of a compass, magnetism is offering people like me, living far north, the pleasure of witnessing the northern lights. The most significant function of magnetism, however, is in redirecting cosmic radiation. Thanks to the field surrounding our planet, the burden of radiation is considerably reduced, which helps us survive.

The Universe presumably contains billions and billions of planets. Do some of them share the properties of our home—and thus,

Stairs cut into solid rock leading up to the ruins of a Hindu temple at Mamallapuram, India.

possibly, life forms based on more or less the same chemistry? (See Appendix IV: *Is There Anybody Out There?* p. 199, for a discussion.)

Carbon is so unique, and so important for us, that you may well consider it a gift from the Creator of the Universe. Some people appreciate the attributes of carbon in its crystalline form—what we refer to as diamonds. It is said that diamonds last forever, but living organisms are not just larger, but more precious, and more lasting, than any diamond. All life forms (at least on this planet) are based on molecules where carbon is the central element. In other words, carbon has been incorporated in a continuous chain of organic molecules dating back to long before the first diamonds were formed. We all share the Earth's reservoir of carbon, so we are all part of the "diamond" of life.

Plants, as well as many animals, quite often suffer the dubious fate of being eaten alive. Humans are normally able to avoid that—only to be eaten after they die. So when they close the lid on one's coffin, bacteria and fungi will soon start recycling one's carbon to create their progeny of bacterial and fungal cells. By being cremated one cheats these organisms for the party, but the carbon atoms in our bodies are recycled nevertheless; most of it goes up in smoke as carbon dioxide. Actually, most of the carbon does at some point pass through the carbon dioxide stage, but sooner or later it will again find its way back into the world of the living, primarily due to the photosynthetic activity of plants.

What is so special about carbon? A central feature of this element is that each carbon atom can readily bind to four other atoms. This property allows for the formation of complex compounds—what we refer to as organic molecules. The larger molecules, such as proteins and DNA, contain thousands, or even millions, of atoms tied together—mostly carbon, oxygen, nitrogen, and hydrogen. There is an almost infinite potential for creating different molecules, and this variability is what makes life possible. The molecules are shaped and selected to care for the processes taking place inside the cells.

It is interesting to note how carbon is formed in the first place: The stars start their career by fusing hydrogen nuclei to form helium. At a later stage they turn to fusing three helium nuclei in a very particular nuclear reaction, which happens to produce carbon. One might have guessed that the fusion of two helium cores would have been a more likely event—the product would have been the less useful element beryllium—but for reasons we do not fully comprehend the stars prefer to produce carbon.[17]

---

[17] For an account of how carbon is formed, see M. E. Eid, "The Process of Carbon Creation," *Nature* 433 (2005): 117–18.

Several types of organic molecules are formed spontaneously, both on Earth and elsewhere in space. Two of them are of particular significance: amino acids, which are the building blocks of proteins, and bases, which are the main unit of genes (known as nucleic acids, DNA or RNA). Genes and proteins are the key molecular players in the process of life.

Most of the small, organic molecules that occur spontaneously are not representative of those present in living organisms. In other words, life implies an intentional and directed production of specific molecules. Furthermore, life is based on a particular set of principles; the most important of which are those directing the process of evolution.

Evolution implies that there is a guiding code behind the design of all organisms. The process of evolution is rooted in the general rules of chemistry, which again follow the underlying physical laws of the Universe. The process, however, operates on a totally different level compared to the physical laws. Evolution is something special. Even the most genius specialist in physics and cosmology would be unlikely to predict the occurrence of such a process, or its products, based on knowledge about the physical laws; thus, the presence of living organisms is in many ways a big surprise. As a biologist, I do understand how evolution operates, but as a human being I sense a Divine presence standing behind it. (See *Evolution— God's Tool?*, p. 28.)

———

Apparently it took only a few hundred million years for life to start up once the conditions became suitable on Earth. When the planet was first formed, the temperature was above the boiling point, implying that the water was either in an enormous steam cloud or tied up inside rocks. The surface temperature had to cool sufficiently for the vapor to condense and create an ocean. In the beginning there was presumably only one ocean, covering the entire surface of the planet—not because water was more plentiful, but because the Earth's surface was flat. The processes involved in creating havoc—that is, forming mountains—had not yet started.

Going back 4.3 billion years, the ocean had formed, and thus a key prerequisite for life was present.[18] The oldest, reasonably certain signs of life in the form of fossils, date back only 2.7 billion years. It

———

[18] J. Copley, "Proof of Life," *New Scientist* (February 22, 2003): 28–31.

is, however, rather unlikely for early forms of life to make fossils at all; and even if they did, most of the rocks from this period have since vanished. Whatever fossils were there are highly unlikely to be recovered today. Life may date as far back as four billion years, but we are unlikely to recover traces of the first organisms that appeared on earth.

It is conceivable that living cells arose in several places independently of each other, using somewhat different chemical recipes. On the other hand, it is not obvious that there is any alternative to the biochemical recipe of present organisms, with the possible exception of minor modifications. What we do know for sure is that all present life forms are based on the same biochemistry, using proteins and genes as the main players. Thus, for the same reason that we can say that the Universe emerged from a single event, we can say that life arose from a single "seed."

The expression "inside we are all the same" is certainly true at the molecular level—whether you compare individual members of the human race or compare us with bacteria. All cells make use of the same genetic material (DNA and RNA), and basically the same types of chemical reactions. Thus, all forms of life are obviously related; the one and only device that has caused us to drift apart is the process of evolution. Our shared chemistry, however, is also what keeps us together. In fact, we are not just related, we belong together, and we depend on each other. We may very well be described as a single living thing: the planet *Gaia*.

By performing a more detailed analysis of the genetic material we can even create a tree of life encompassing every species. At the root of that tree stands the common ancestor of us all. In biology, however, we do not use the names Adam and Eve, but prefer to refer to our shared ancestor as LUCA. LUCA is short for the "Last Universal Common Ancestor"—that is, the progenitor of all present-day life forms. LUCA did not reproduce sexually, thus the terms "forefather" or "foremother" would be equally invalid. In fact, LUCA presumably resembles present-day bacteria.[19] (See Figure 6: *LUCA—A Portrait,* next page.)

---

[19] G. Hamilton, "Mother Superior," *New Scientist* (September 3, 2005): 26–29.

LUCA—A Portrait

We assume that LUCA, the shared ancestor of all living organisms, originated in hot springs; and that it resembled a simplified version of present bacteria. Bacterial life forms are common in today's hot springs. Some of them still obtain their energy from chemical reactions involving minerals; they are self-sufficient—needing neither sunlight nor food produced by other forms of life, as was necessary for the first life forms on Earth.[20]

LUCA, however, must have been somewhat different from the modern version of "mineral eaters." Hot-spring lovers like to be where it is hottest; they live in water close to the boiling point. LUCA more likely lived away from the worst heat, as it requires advanced strategies to prevent cells from being destroyed in near boiling water. Thus, the present inhabitants of hot springs have adapted to this sort of life more recently.

While all life forms around today (some viruses excluded) use DNA to store their genes, the very first forms of life probably used RNA molecules instead. At some point life came to prefer the use of DNA. DNA is almost similar to RNA, but has a more stable structure, thus offering safer storage. RNA has, on the other hand, the advantage that it can both serve as storage for genetic information and at the same time do actual "work" in the cell; that is, RNA may have played the role of proteins.

Life is presently based on the principle that DNA serves as a blueprint for the production of proteins, while it is the task of the proteins to ensure that what needs to be done is done. Theoretically, it may be possible to build living cells without proteins. Such cells would consist of self-replicating RNA, a lipid substance to form a surrounding membrane, and a mixture of small organic molecules needed to synthesize the former two. However, as all present cells make use of DNA, so did most likely LUCA, implying that "RNA only" cells, if they ever existed, became extinct prior to the days of LUCA.

---

[20] The Tree of Life is divided into three domains: *Eubacteria, Archaea,* and *Eukarya.* The former two are both "bacteria-like" and thus here loosely referred to as bacteria; however, some scientists believe that LUCA was more closely related to *Archaea* than to the true bacteria of today.

How LUCA came to exist is the one point in biology that is the most difficult to understand. We have models that offer reasonable explanations for what happened afterward—that is to say, onward to the evolution of multi-cellular organisms and the existence of intelligent life—but the assembly of a living cell from scratch is almost impossible to envision. Accordingly, it is tempting to include Divine intervention as one of the required ingredients; however, that does not stop us from trying to understand what might have happened—without resorting to Divine Providence.[21]

Perhaps, if we are ever successful in this task, we just might have an idea how God operates.

As mentioned previously, some of the chemical building blocks that life depends on could easily crop up through non-biological processes in the early ocean. The difficult part is the next step: The possibility of having a living cell assemble spontaneously with these building blocks has been compared to putting a computer keyboard in front of a gorilla. The gorilla will probably push some of the buttons and be fascinated by the concomitant response on the screen; but the probability of having random organic molecules assemble into a viable cell is presumably on the order of magnitude of having the gorilla complete a sensible novel.

At least five ingredients are required to generate life:
1. A set of chemical elements present in the form of very simple molecules such as: methane (CH_4), ammonia (NH_3), hydrogen sulfide (H_2S), carbon dioxide (CO_2), and phosphate (PO_4^{3-}).
2. These molecules must combine to form slightly more complex organic molecules.
3. All the molecules must be present in an appropriate solvent.
4. The molecules must be enriched in a restricted area.
5. In the same area there must be a suitable source of energy used to further combine and restructure the above mentioned building blocks into the considerably more complex molecules of life.

---

[21] For more comprehensive accounts of how life might have started, see for example, J. W. Schopf, *Life's Origin: The Beginnings of Biological Evolution* (2002); R. M. Hazen, *Genesis: The Scientific Quest for Life's Origins* (2005); or C. de Duve, *Singularities: Landmarks on the Pathway to Life* (2005).

Combining these ingredients and waiting a few hundred million years may yield a similar situation to that which existed on Earth and led to the evolution of life. A prayer may help speed up the process.

Here on Earth there is one solvent suitable for life: water (H_2O). Theoretically, it might be possible to use other fluids, such as liquid ammonia, but water is definitely preferable. Moreover, as water is formed spontaneously by mixing hydrogen and oxygen, which are two of the most common elements in the Universe, it is a reasonable guess that life on other planets, if it exists, is also based on water.

In the form of smaller molecules, the required building blocks may have been present all over the original ocean, but the final two ingredients would only be available at selected locations: Life required an energy source to be present in a restricted area that allowed for the accumulation of building blocks.

The crust of the Earth is thin; if the planet is compared to an egg, the crust is thinner than the eggshell. Consequently, the molten rock of the underlying mantle sometimes presses through the crust and erupts on the surface—as in a volcano. On the young Earth, volcanic activity was presumably rare, because the crust was reasonably intact, but then, as now, a related phenomenon was probably common: On areas where the crust is particularly thin, we find geysers or hot springs. These occur on dry land, but also at the bottom of the sea. They form wherever water seeps sufficiently far down into the ground to come across hot rocks or magma. The subsequent heating causes the water to evaporate, and the concomitant expansion forces vapor, as well as the water trapped above, up to the surface.

The island of Iceland, which is located in an area with lots of volcanic activity, has ample amounts of free hot water due to hot springs. Hot water is in itself not worth much for the purpose of generating life, but the actual key rests with a minor detail: The rising water is rich in minerals. As any decent cook can verify, hot water is a better solvent compared to cold water; thus, minerals are added while the water circulates in the crust. The dissolved minerals happen to take care of two crucial functions:

One of those functions concerns the fact that certain combinations of minerals are a source of chemical energy. It is a question of a type of chemical activity referred to as reduction-oxidation reactions. The relevant minerals—for example, salts of iron and sulfur—are dissolved in the hot water and are probably the original source of energy for life.[22]

In order to synthesize complex molecules, however, it is not sufficient to have energy; one also needs a mechanism by which the energy can be harnessed. The situation is somewhat like driving a car: The wheels do not move just because you burn fuel in the cylinders; there has to be a device that transfers the power. Living cells have advanced procedures for this purpose. The production of early, organic molecules using the energy of the minerals probably had to rely on primitive catalysts that worked in a more arbitrary fashion. For random processes to come up with anything interesting, it is essential that the organic molecules accumulate at a specific spot, which brings us to the second function of the minerals: erecting a "house."

The oceans are enormous, and there are constant currents dispersing whatever molecules of interest might emerge. Consequently, it is difficult to obtain a high concentration of anything in open water. Fortunately, the hot springs create a form of compartments. Some of the minerals dissolved in the hot water will precipitate when cooled down, forming structures on the floor of the ocean. We still find "chimneys" erected in this way by hydrothermal vents, and some may stand 10 or 20 meters tall. The important point is that, due to the way they are formed, the chimneys are porous, i.e., there are tiny compartments all over the otherwise solid structure. These pores may have offered the first shelter, or containment, for nascent life on Earth, possible augmented by foamy bubbles that typically form in water rich in iron and sulphur.[23]

---

[22] Actually, most of the chemical processes taking place inside a cell are oxidative reactions, but they typically involve the oxidation or reduction of carbon. In this type of reaction, chemical energy is released during the transfer of electrons between atoms. The clue here is how to harness similar reactions between non-organic minerals in order to transfer the energy to organic compounds. See N. Lane, "The Cradle of Life," *New Scientist* (October 17, 2009): 38–42.

[23] For further discussion, see E. V. Koonin and W. Martin, "On the Origin of Genomes and Cells Within Inorganic Compartments," *Trends in Genetics* 21 (2005): 647–654; and A. Ricardo and J. W. Szostak, "Life on Earth," *Scientific American* (September 2009): 38–45.

Presumably it was possible to create a reasonably thick soup of organic molecules within these pores or bubbles. The next step may have been the initiation of various chemical processes, which gradually produced even more advanced compounds. Eventually there may have appeared small proteins, as well as genetic material in the form of RNA. Yet, we are still talking about a lifeless soup. It is the step moving from an advanced soup to an actual living cell that is so hard to explain.

Cells need a guiding principle—that is to say, a machinery with the capacity to make sure the required molecules are produced at the correct time and at the right spot within the cell. All cells use pretty much the same sort of machinery for this purpose. The governing principle is that genetic material directs the production of proteins and that the proteins subsequently take care of the various processes required for life to flourish. The concept is reasonably simple, yet ingeniously conceived. We understand how it can sustain an independent replicative unit in the form of a cell; we just do not understand how it came about in the first place.

Another problem with respect to the creation of cellular life is that all cells are contained within a membrane composed primarily of fatty acids. These membranes are highly practical in that they retain the soup of life, but at the same time they permit the import of nutrients and the export of waste. Furthermore, they allow the cell to divide into two equal daughter cells once it has grown sufficiently large. The mineral pores or bubbles may have served the purpose of containment, but they are quite useless for these other purposes. Again, the point is that we know in detail how cellular membranes function, but it is difficult to explain how they were first established.

Life on Earth does not disappear just because we are unable to explain how it got started. There has to be an explanation. The unsuccessful struggle to find a scientific account, however, makes it tempting to suggest that a sixth component was required: a helping hand from a Divine force.

If by means of a time machine, you could go back to the time of early life, you would be in for a nasty surprise. You would be destined to a reasonably swift, but not very comfortable, death—by suffocation. In those days there was no oxygen in the atmosphere; if there had been oxygen, there would probably never have been any LUCA—or us. Oxygen was highly toxic to early life, as it still is for a considerable number of bacteria. This is because oxygen tends to react with, and thus break down, organic molecules. Organisms exposed to air, as we are, have particular systems protecting our molecules. Several of the bacteria harbored in your gut, or in the deeper corners of your mouth, are less fortunate; they die if brought out into the open.

At first the atmosphere presumably consisted of carbon dioxide, water vapor, and nitrogen. Most of the vapor eventually became ocean, and a considerable fraction of the carbon dioxide was either dissolved in water or precipitated as minerals, primarily in the form of calcium carbonate. Nitrogen consequently became the main component of the atmosphere, as it still is. The situation was perfect for life in those days, but as a human you might as well have tried living on Mars.

After several hundred million years, there arose a novel form of life: photosynthesizing organisms. They were not like plants such as those one finds outside, but bacterial cells mastering the art of converting solar energy into the production of organic matter. Their development had crucial consequences. The effect was overwhelming. One of the greatest leaps of progress the Earth has ever witnessed. Life on Earth was literarily "turned loose," i.e., the cells were released from a sole presence around hydrothermal vents. Photosynthetic life could live wherever the sun was shining, which meant anywhere in the upper part of the sea. Life passed from a rare "freak show" to a global ecosystem.

The emergence of photosynthesis had another profound effect. Photosynthetic life probably began some 3 billion years ago, but in the early forms the procedure for utilizing sunlight was somewhat primitive. Soon, however, there evolved the type of photosynthesis used by the trees and flowers that exist today. This process produces oxygen (O_2). We know that oxygen appeared in the atmosphere between 2.5 and 3 billion years ago, and that the only procedure capable of putting it there is photosynthesis. The Earth was never again the same.[24]

---

[24] J. F. Allen and W. Martin, "Out of Thin Air," *Nature* 445 (2007): 610–12.

As mentioned above, oxygen is potentially poisonous; thus, this evolutionary stride was a daring experiment. On the other hand, once the organisms had evolved a means to control the situation—that is, installed the necessary protection—oxygen offered an opportunity that life simply could not afford to miss: The combustion of organic molecules could be made 18 times more efficient. Consider a car manufacturer designing a car that will travel 18 times the distance of previous models on the same amount of gasoline. It will be an immediate success. The same was the case for those organisms managing to harness the combustion of carbon sources by means of oxygen. They prospered. Not surprisingly, most present cells, including all higher life forms, have "engines" containing the relevant contraption.

Photosynthesis thus enabled life to take two giant leaps forward: first, by allowing organisms to spread out; and second, by offering a faster and more efficient way of living. Actually, there was a third, and possibly even more important, consequence. The emergence of photosynthesis opened novel niches in nature, and thus enabled a larger variety of life forms to evolve. Prior to photosynthesis, most organisms were probably doing pretty much the same thing. By creating a larger span of opportunities—for example, in the form of eating plants rather than being self-sufficient. Photosynthesis helped speed up the process of evolution.

The next giant leap for promoting life on Earth was the appearance of a more complex type of cells, what we call eukaryotic life forms; and then to make these cells cooperate by forming multicellular organisms. All organisms visible to the naked eye are the product of these two innovations. (See *Life the Way You See It*, below.[25])

Life the Way You See It

Bacteria are ubiquitous. In competition with viruses, they are the Earth's first and foremost success story, but they have one weakness—they remain small.

For the first two billion years or so, bacterial cells were presumably alone on the planet. Then, something strange happened: an

---

[25] R. Dawkins offers an excellent account of the evolution of life in *The Ancestor's Tale: A Pilgrimage to the Dawn of Evolution* (2004).

incident that formed the basis for higher life forms. One cell made a very smart move. Instead of simply eating fellow bacteria, this cell took another bacterium as a tenant—without killing it. Somewhat like Jonah surviving inside the stomach of the whale, but on a considerably smaller scale. Such an event seems very unlikely, both in terms of bacteria and whales, but in the case of bacteria it must have occurred at least twice. On two occasions cells that were engulfed alive gradually transformed into something very useful.

In one case a regular bacterium with the capacity to utilize oxygen was slowly reshaped by evolution into what is referred to as mitochondria, which today are vital components of all advanced cells. Cells containing mitochondria are referred to as eukaryotic cells—in contrast to bacteria-like cells. All higher organisms—that is, all plants and animals—are made of eukaryotic cells. The mitochondria are the "engines" that stand for much of the energy production in these cells.

Then, on a second occasion one of the newly formed eukaryotic cells repeated the success, but this time by swallowing a photosynthesizing bacterium. It became the part of the plant cells that are called chloroplasts. The chloroplasts are responsible for photosynthesis in plants.

What nature did was to combine different independent life forms to create new super cells, and what made these events so important was that they allowed for more advanced types of life. Everything you can see with the naked eye—as well as a considerable variety of microscopic life—is the result of the merger of these bacterial cells. In fact, these events are considered to be among the most important inventions ever made by the process of evolution, primarily because the eukaryotic cells turned out to be sufficiently advanced to set up extensive collaborations: They formed multicellular organisms. The evolutionary process subsequently lost all inhibition.

Multicellular life has two significant advantages. They can grow large and thus dominate lesser life forms; and, more importantly, they can do what is so highly valued in human society: division of labor. It implies that each cell specialize in particular functions. Your body, for example, is an assembly of an enormous variety of cells, including nerve cells, blood cells, and liver cells. The creation of multicellular life was another astonishing event.

The course required for the evolution of human beings has taken a very long time indeed, presumably close to four billion years. Most of the time evolution moved forward slowly and painstakingly, much as a slug going up a steep hill, but at certain points the slug suddenly made giant leaps forward. The emergence of photosynthesis and multicellular life caused such leaps, but the most visible jump occurred around 530 million years ago. What happened then is referred to as the *Cambrian explosion*. It appears as if evolution went wild. Based on the fossil record, within a few million years all sorts of weird life forms appeared.

The strange thing is that all the different phyla of animals appear to have evolved at about the same time; that is to say, the oldest known fossils of the forty or so strategies evolution has devised for animal life date back to the very same period. Though life was still confined to the sea, all present-day animals can trace their ancestry back to the Cambrian Ocean. It is as if the Creator had a particularly busy day at work. The ensuing job was primarily to trim the strategies worth taking care of, and to weed out the rest.

Gradually life crept out of the sea. The plants presumably came first; after all, the life-giving rays of the sun shine stronger on dry land compared to beneath the surface of the ocean. Moreover, without plants, land did not have much to offer animals, but as the plants showed the way, a whole set of novel opportunities arose. Evolution did not miss this chance, so pretty soon the terrain was teeming with all sorts of life. (See *Eyes and Brain—Your Most Important Asset,* below.)

Eyes and Brain—Your Most Important Assets

The eyes and the brain are the two most wonderful devices formed by evolution—at least as seen by humans. Both probably date back to just before the "Cambrian explosion," some 535 million years ago, when animal life in the sea exploded in all possible directions. Life was able to do without eyes and brain for three billion years, which means it was not obvious that they should emerge.

Today there are many versions of the visual organ. Mammalian eyes, for example, are of a completely different construction when compared to those of insects or snails. Yet, the ability to perceive light probably has a common origin in the form of photosensitive areas of the skin. Similarly, all brains can be traced back to simple nerve circuits of early multicellular organisms. The brilliance of these two devices is that the eyes provide important information about the environment, while the nervous system makes it possible to react to that information, if only in the form of directed movement.

It has been argued that the road to the heart of a man is through his mouth. The assertion is almost correct. The minor mistake is that it does not end up in the heart, but instead in the brain. And that is fortunate. It is the brain that one really wants to influence. (The heart has about as much impact on a man's feelings and actions as his big toe.)

The most important task for the first brain-like neural systems, and perhaps for present brains as well, was to find food. Consequently, in all animals the brain and the mouth are situated close to each other. The early nervous systems were minimal collections of nerve cells surrounding the mouth. In combination with the eyes, also conveniently located in the same area, they gave an enormous benefit in the form of more efficient foraging. Besides leading the body toward a food source, the brain eventually developed another feature—memory—which made it possible to remember where a particular food source is located, and to make educated guesses based on environmental clues as to where to find more. The animals that developed these benefits were sure to prosper. Consequently, evolution went into high gear. The three phyla of animals that presently dominate the Earth are all descendants of species that developed vision and brain: vertebrates, arthropods (insects and crustaceans), and mollusks (snails, shellfish, and octopus).

Plants need neither brain nor eyes. They remain where they have set down roots and take the world as it comes. Then again, when life depends primarily on sunlight, moving toward the food source means growing tall, a challenge that does not require extensive thinking.

The most successful group, or phylum, of animals, at least in terms of number of species, is the arthropods. They include insects and spiders as well as shellfish such as crabs and shrimps. This phylum was probably among the first to colonize land. Fortunately, land-living arthropods cannot grow large. Their anatomy restricts their size, primarily because they lack lungs; instead, they obtain oxygen through open channels branching off into their bodies. If the body became too big, oxygen would not reach the inner parts. They compensate for this, however, by forming a large number of individuals; some species actually create giant "super individuals" by extreme forms of social cooperation, as in an anthill. There can be millions of ants in an anthill, and they function more or less like a single organism.

We belong to the vertebrates, a phylum that started off with fish. Some 360 million years ago fish that lived in shallow waters developed their fins in the direction of a device useful for crawling. The change gave them the opportunity to creep onto dry land and thus feed on the foodstuff available there. The idea was a hit in the sense that evolution continued this line of development and ended up with a range of amphibians, including frogs and toads. One more step forward and reptiles, such as the dinosaurs, appeared—the most grandiose and dramatic animals ever to be seen on dry land. Another stride, which started 200 million years ago, gave rise to mammals.

The early mammals were, in principle, a considerable improvement compared to reptiles. Mammals are warm-blooded, which means they can live under more varied climatic conditions, while reptiles turn sluggish when the temperature falls. The mammals also have more advanced brains. Yet, the early forms of mammals were not an immediate success in spite of their apparent advantages; they remained small and insignificant like shrews. The dinosaurs ruled land, while our ancestors were hiding under rocks and branches in an endless struggle to avoid becoming food for the rulers.

The situation remained like this for almost 150 million years. In those days land was already covered by plants mixed with a rich variety of animals. The reptiles even conquered the air by evolving flying forms, and eventually became the progenitors of the present-day birds.

Other reptiles just increased in size. Evolution typically performs that trick on flourishing species. As usual, the plant eaters increased the most, as they had the most to lose by being small compared to attacking predators. Some of the predators were certainly big enough. For example, the renowned sauropods reached a length of 40m and a height of 18m, and the most notorious one, *Tyranno-*

saurus rex, could stand up to 13m tall, with teeth like a crocodile and jaws big enough to crush a human without spilling blood on the chin.

Our ancestors would probably have remained small, scared and insignificant if fate had not, literally, struck. About 65 million years ago, life on Earth experienced possibly the worst catastrophe ever. This catastrophe, however, is likely to have been our salvation. One, or possibly several, asteroids or comets hit the planet; the biggest chunk most likely somewhere between Yucatan and Texas. The collision shook the entire planet, but the worst part was the dust thrown up from the impact and the fires that further filled the air with particles. Consequently, the sun disappeared from view and the temperature dropped several degrees. As a secondary consequence, plants died and with them the animals that either directly or indirectly depended on plants for food.

Large animals are more vulnerable to this sort of cataclysm compared to small animals, the cold-blooded more vulnerable than the warm-blooded. Apparently, all animals larger than the size of cats disappeared from dry land. Fortunately, our ancestors were still small.

———

As the plants gradually recovered from the slump, opportunities waited for those who survived. The sudden availability of novel niches speeded up evolution; thus the mammals branched out into a variety of new forms, and, as with other successful species, many of them became larger. Today they dominate life on land. The roles have changed. Most present-day reptiles are small and easily scared, such as the lizards running for shelter at the slightest movement of your hand.

———

We can paint a likely scenario detailing how the evolutionary process moved from bacteria all the way to human beings. However, the process not only required some four billion years; it also demanded a series of epoch-making incidents—in the form of rather strange and surprising twists of fate.[26]

I have discussed some of these, such as the development of photosynthesis, and the collision with an asteroid or a comet.

———

[26] To learn a bit more about these incidents, see C. Ainsworth et al., "Life's Greatest Inventions," *New Scientist* (April 9, 2005): 27–35; or N. Lane, *Life Ascending: The Ten Great Inventions of Evolution* (2009).

We tend to take for granted all the events contributing to the evolution of our species; after all, the product is here for all to see and experience. Nonetheless, if we delve into the details of what happened, it is not just weird, but extraordinary. The path toward advanced organisms depended not only on surprising biological innovations but also on some rather unique and peculiar physical features of our planet.

I have pointed out that Earth consists of a thin crust covering the molten magma of the mantle. One feature that few people ponder is that this crust has just the right thickness. It is sufficiently solid to offer reasonable stability to life on the surface, but at the same time thin enough for two important processes to take place: One is the occurrence of hydrothermal vents, which presumably was required for life to begin; the other is to make sure the surface is not just flat and boring. If everything is covered with water, there is not much chance for evolution to create life on land; thus, our existence depended on a process capable of erecting mountains—not just for the purpose of having dry ground, but to create a diversity of environmental conditions. The evolutionary process is at its most innovative when life is forced to adapt to ever-altering circumstances.

In the beginning, our planet was presumably a rather boring place, geologically speaking. However, at some point, perhaps after a billion years, things started to happen. Volcanic activity divided the crust into large plates that began to drift around—a process referred to as plate tectonics or continental drift. Where the plates collide, mountains arise. The process gave the Earth not only continents, but a variety of climatic zones and geographic diversity.[27]

Some 200 million years ago, all the land masses were gathered in one giant supercontinent referred to as Pangaea. Then Pangaea broke up into the continents we have today. The division of continents meant that various forms of life could evolve independently in different regions, which again added to the diversity of life forms. Only those species on which evolution managed to use its full potential for creating modifications survived. In other words, the instability of the land masses oiled the process of evolution that transitioned into ever more advanced life forms. (See *Tools of Evolution: Sex and Death,* next page.)

---

[27] A. Witze, "The Start of the World as We Know It," *Nature* 442 (2006): 128–31.

Tools of Evolution: Sex and Death

The first living cells reproduced simply by dividing in two. They had no sex life and were not destined to die. Death occurred when, due to adverse luck, they ended up in places that would not support life. Back then life was sweet and simple.

The capacity for genetic exchange between cells was perhaps the first—and most crucial—upgrade of life. Swapping genes makes evolution a lot more efficient. It offers the opportunity to combine the best qualities from two different cells into one superior organism. The mixing of genes is, however, a random process, which implies that many cells are unfortunate and end up with a collection of useless genes. That doesn't matter. The unsuitable versions simply die. It is much more important to create one cell with enhanced properties—perhaps only one out of thousands of cells sharing genes—because that one cell can multiply and thus pass on the good genes.

Today, bacteria have developed sophisticated ways to obtain genes from other cells. In multicellular forms of life, the primary method is what we refer to as sex: Typically there are two types of individuals (referred to as mating types or genders, and in some species there are actually more than two): Man and Woman if you happen to be a human. Gametes from the two fuse, and a new individual with a random pick of genes from mother and father is born.

It would be a lot easier, and more efficient, to drop sex and instead practice virgin birth. Aphids go on like that all summer. The offspring are pregnant with the next generation even before they are born. But when autumn comes, the aphids seek a mate and procreate sexually—for the reason that, without the occasional mixing of genes, the species risk getting stuck in an evolutionary dead end, where the accumulation of harmful mutations causes the line of descent to deteriorate. So no matter how clumsy one might consider the option of sex to be, it had, and still has, an important role in the evolution of complex life forms—including us.

Death is another factor that helps evolution progress. Aging is in our genes. We gradually slip into a process that ends with our demise. Some trees live for thousands of years, and it probably would have been possible for evolution to design a Methuselah race of humans, but it would have slowed down the process. Consequently, we are not designed to live for more than a hundred years.

Human individuals presently need to give way for newer and, hopefully, slightly better versions, because only in that way can the species adapt to constantly changing living conditions and thus survive in competition with other species.

Both sex and death are, in other words, important tools for evolution. Without them, the process would most likely not have brought forth human beings. The cost—aging, venereal diseases, and frustration—is probably worth the price.

I have not yet entered into the most incredible chapter in the tale of life. The evolution of mankind is the part we know best; yet it includes some of the most astonishing aspects of the story. Perhaps we are not that big, or that much to look at, but our brain is the most fantastic contraption evolution has ever come up with. To produce living cells was a miracle, but to create a life form with the capacity to understand the Universe is an even more spectacular achievement. Then again, it did not take that much time to produce life, but it took some four billion years to construct profound intelligence.

A Unique Species

According to legend, the aphorism "Know thyself" was inscribed in stone at the entrance to the temple of Delphi. It is, in my mind, a very sensible inscription. It is indeed useful to know our evolutionary history, because by understanding how this process has shaped us, we can create a template for understanding ourselves.[28]

Out of the myriad of opportunities following the decline and fall of the dinosaurs, early forms of an order of animals known as primates emerged. The primates eventually diverged into prosimians, monkeys, and apes—the latter being our closest relatives on the Tree of Life. The early primates had keen vision, presumably due to being active at night when daytime was occupied by dangerous dinosaurs. They were also good climbers, but otherwise they probably did not possess any obvious features that might suggest a potential

---

[28] Here there is only space for a short introduction. In a previous book, *Darwinian Happiness* (2002), I offer a more detailed discussion about our innate qualities.

for evolving spectacular qualities. Today there are some 400 species of primates remaining, but as a group they are not particularly successful: Most of the species are rare, and about half are considered in danger of extinction, with one obvious exception—us.[29]

We belong to the family of apes. The ancestral ape split with the monkeys about 30 million years ago. At that point they probably lived in Africa, but much of the subsequent evolutionary history of apes may actually have taken place in Asia. In fact, most of the present species still live there: the orangutans, gibbons, and siamangs. However, our closest relatives, the bonobos, chimpanzees, and gorillas, moved at some point back to Africa. Thus, the unique human characteristics were presumably shaped on the sea shores and open forest landscapes of the continent of Africa.

At one point the apes were actually a rather successful group. They included a considerable variety of species, some standing more than three meters tall. Then, about ten million years ago, things got worse. Most of the species became extinct.[30]

Fruit was presumably an important part of the diet for early apes. One predicament that caused problems may have been that some monkeys began to "cheat"; that is, they evolved the capacity to digest unripe fruit. Prior to becoming ripe, most fruits contain considerable amounts of tannic acids, which apes and humans do not tolerate well. Presumably the apes were bigger and stronger than their monkey cousins, and thus capable of defending fruit trees, but that did not help them when the fruit was gone before it became worth defending.

Fortunately, the branch of apes leading toward humans managed to survive. Approximately five to six million years ago it split off: first from the gorilla and soon thereafter from the chimpanzees and bonobos. The last stage of our evolutionary history had begun.

Early forms of human-like apes were probably no immediate success. Over the last five million years there have been several sprouts from our branch, creatures not that different from us, but all except one of them, *Homo sapiens*, have gone extinct! *Homo neanderthalensis*, for example, parted with our predecessor only half a million years ago and considerable collections of remains have been

---

[29] See R. Dunbar and L. Barrett, *Cousins: Our Primate Relatives* (2000).
[30] D. R. Begun, "Planet of the Apes," *Scientific American* (August 2003): 64–73.

found, suggesting that they were flourishing until recently; yet, they suddenly disappeared 28,000 years ago. We do not know why they did not make it, but we do know that they lived alongside modern humans in Western Europe for at least 10,000 years; and we know that the surviving species has a propensity for aggressive behavior.[31]

Homo floresiensis (nicknamed "the hobbits" due to their small size), whose remnants were recently discovered on the island of Flores in Indonesia, died out as recently as 10,000 years ago.[32]

The earliest species that are considered sufficiently close to us to be awarded the name *Homo*, i.e., human, appeared 2.5- to 3-million years ago. The two more renowned branches are referred to as *Homo erectus* and *Homo habilis*. They lived primarily in Africa, but *Homo erectus* did spread to Asia; in fact, they may still have been present there upon the arrival of the first modern humans some 60,000 years ago—implying that they too may have encountered our ancestors. As in the case of the Neandertals, the dissemination and long-term survival of *Homo erectus* suggest that they were well adapted; yet, unfortunately, they did not quite make it.

Our species, modern humans, have been around for 200,000 years. For a considerable time our forebears presumably fought for their existence as an insignificant group on the border of extinction; moreover, even upon acquiring an advanced human intellect we were not an immediate sensation. The tribes roaming the savannahs of Africa 200,000 years ago had pretty much the same qualities, the same stature, and same intelligence as the present population; yet, they remained an insignificant population. Only after another 100,000 years or so did things start to happen.[33]

We consider ourselves to be a unique species with qualities far superior to those of other primates, not to mention other mammals. It seems strange, therefore, that our ancestors were on the verge of annihilation most of the time. They were only a tiny twig, easily

---

[31] Those interested in the demise of the Neandertals can read K. Wong, "Twilight of the Neandertals," *Scientific American* (August 2009): 34–39.

[32] K. Wong, "The Littlest Human," *Scientific American* (February 2005): 40–49.

[33] See, for example, S. B. Carroll, "Genetics and the Making of Homo Sapiens," *Nature* 422 (2003): 849–57; or D. Garrigan and M. F. Hammer, "Reconstructing Human Origins in the Genomic Era," *Nature Review Genetics* 7 (2006): 669–80.

broken, on the enormous Tree of Life. Then suddenly, within a blink of an eye in terms of an evolutionary time frame, we conquered the Earth. The present situation cannot be explained solely in terms of an evolutionary development, since we obtained our position as "king of the planet" without any concomitant change in our genetic constitution. As a biologist I cannot help wondering how, or why, we suddenly reached our present position.

———

We are able to offer a reasonable narrative, however, as to how or why evolution added key human features to our species. I would begin that story by going back ten million years. In those days our ancestors lived primarily in trees, like present-day orangutans. They moved around either hanging from their arms or balancing on branches with support from their hands.[34]

Eventually they gave up the trees, favoring life in a more open landscape, but their history as tree-dwellers meant that their hind legs became more important for locomotion than their forelegs. At some point, maybe four million years ago, our ancestors started walking upright on two legs, freeing their hands for other purposes. Their hands were already quite versatile, equipped with long fingers capable of grasping and holding on to branches, as well as picking fruits and other edible items such as insects—the perfect starting point for evolution to perform one of its wonders. The delicate motor control of their fingers developed even further, which gave us the capacity to construct tools. Concomitantly, the brain expanded, allowing for gradually more advanced tools.

We are not unique in making tools. Other animals, including the chimpanzees, do so too—although certainly not so well as we do. In fact, we are the only species making tools for the purpose of generating other tools; for example, three million years ago humans were already shaping stones to be used to prepare hides taken from prey. The skin then provided a covering to help keep them warm.

At about the same time, we presumably learned to control fire, which marked the start of culinary art. A Stone Age kitchen would probably not be any immediate success if it opened next to a McDonald's, but being able to cook food means a lot more than just gastronomic delight: The heat makes nutrients more available for

---

[34] P. O'Higgins and S. Elton, "Walking on Trees," *Science* 316 (2007): 1292–94.

the human digestive system. In other words, by mastering fire our ancestors were able to extract more calories with no more effort than that used in obtaining foodstuff. Furthermore, cooking may also have boosted sociability, since it became practical to cook and eat together around a shared fire.[35]

Compared to size, no other organisms have a body as expensive to operate as we humans, primarily because our brain is such a costly contraption. In a resting adult, the brain demands 25% of the energy consumed; in infants the percentage is closer to 60%. In a way, this is an unfair allocation of resources as the brain only constitutes 2% and 10% of the body weight in adults and infants respectively. We managed to get hold of the amount of calories required to feed our expensive brains by learning to hunt, because meat offers more concentrated food than plants, and learning to cook food improved digestion. Thus, fire was presumably an important step in that it paved the way for the creation of a more complex brain.[36]

The use of tools, combined with advanced forms of social collaboration, such as when hunting in a group, were influential in driving evolution toward another crucial human characteristic—that of culture.

Culture implies the transfer of obtained knowledge from one generation to the next. Again, other animals including chimpanzees have culture. For example, chimpanzees teach their offspring to use tools, such as the "fishing rods" they stick into termite mounds to obtain a mouthful of termites. In other animals, however, culture is less important for daily living. We are unique in that most of our activities rely heavily on cultural transmission of knowledge. The extraordinary fountain of information possessed by mankind is what makes the advancement of human pursuits possible, but even in the Stone Age there is no doubt that tribes who managed to retain and expand relevant knowledge had a considerable advantage. Moreover, cultural transmission was presumably a driving force toward the development of elaborate verbal communication, because language makes teaching others so much easier. Yet, the most important facet of recent human evolution may have been that we became a highly

---

[35] W. R. Leonard, "Food for Thought. Dietary Change Was a Driving Force in Human Evolution," *Scientific American* (December 2002): 75–83.
[36] A. Gibbons, "Food for Thought," *Science* 316 (2007): 1558–60.

gregarious animal. The advantages of cooperation led to the intricacies and challenges of social life. In fact, community-living was most likely crucial for adding the final touch to human mental powers. (See *The Social Sense*, below.)

The Social Sense

Altruistic social behavior is by no means obvious. Indeed, as a biological phenomenon it is rather strange. Although it seems appropriate to have parents collaborate in caring for their progeny, cooperation among adults of the same sex is bizarre. The rule of thumb says that they should fight and compete with each other.

Then again, if you happen to be with close relatives, the genes might want you to lend a hand. After all, your relatives carry many of the same genes you have; thus, it is in the interest of the shared genes to help each other, which is really only an extension of the principle that parents ought to care for their offspring.

Humans are surprisingly social; yet we are far from being the most social species on Earth. Those who deserve this award, such as bees and ants, operate by the principle of helping close relatives. This tenet has presumably played an important role in the evolution of social life in humans as well, but we appear to have in us the capacity for more kindness than what one would expect the genes to wish for: Not only do we help unrelated people, we even help total strangers. In fact, evolution has played on a more varied register in order to shape this sort of social behavior.

Reciprocity is one important component. The term implies that we help one another because those who benefit are expected to help us later. The principle may be extended to work indirectly: I help you in order to obtain a good reputation in the community, thereby making it more likely that others will help me. The more controversial notion of group selection may have further boosted our geniality. Group selection means that I am inclined to help others who belong to my group—whether they are related or not—because if the group does well, so do I.[37]

---

[37] For more on the evolution of social behaviour and on group selection, see D. S. Wilson and E. O. Wilson, "Rethinking the Theoretical Foundation of Sociobiology," *The Quarterly Review of Biology* 82 (2007): 327–48.

It may be asked, Why help the poor people of Africa or earthquake survivors in Indonesia or Haiti or elsewhere around the globe?

The answer is that, genetically, we are not supposed to. However, our capacity for compassion and empathy are coupled with brain rewards—it feels good to be kind. During the formative part of our evolutionary history, strangers were rare, and those you did meet were potential allies. Thus, there was no reason to restrict the rewards of compassion to a select few; instead, the rewards can be accessed by whomever you choose to be kind to. Anyone who cares for the future of the human race should rejoice at this apparent forethought of evolution.

There is a reasonably distinct correlation between the size of the brain of various species of animals and how complex their social life is.[38] Presumably interacting with other members of our species requires not just shrewdness, but a considerable intellectual effort. Advanced communication is taxing, and on top of that you need to be able to read subtle signals in the voice and expressions of others that enable you to evaluate their feelings and intentions. These two facets of human nature, language and social relations, probably laid the foundations for the most impressive—and most frightening— achievement of the evolutionary process: Our species has, by means of its intellect, managed to take control of the entire planet.

Apparently the human population in Africa was in great shape 100,000 years ago. Perhaps at that point our forebears had become more clever about exploiting their intellect and coping with the conditions offered by the environment—spurred more by the advancement of culture than by changes in their genes. What we know is that they started to migrate to other parts of the world. Territory may have become a limiting resource, possibly because a large fraction of the population preferred to make a living by the ocean and good seafront property is scarce. There is indeed evidence suggesting that humans for a period of their evolutionary history lived by, and off, the sea. Moreover, at that time we presumably

---

[38] R. I. M. Dunbar and S. Shultz, "Evolution in the Social Brain," *Science* 317 (2007): 1344–46.

mastered not just swimming, but also the art of building simple boats; thus, expansion along the coastlines was relatively easy. Unfortunately, it is difficult to find evidence for ancient beach life because the water level is much higher today, and underwater excavations are rather difficult.

What we do know is that over the next 50,000 years humans spread to Europe, Australia, and as far away as the eastern parts of Asia. Then, maybe 20,000 years ago, they managed to cross the Bering Strait to Alaska, where they did not stop but continued right down to the end of South America. Our species had conquered all the continents except Antarctica.

Biologically speaking we are, without doubt, an enormous success—at least for the time being. More than six billion individuals should give the human genes every reason to rejoice. Then again, biological success is typically measured as the total biomass of all individuals belonging to a particular species; and based on that principle we are only a good number two. The current winner is the Antarctic krill, *Euphausia superba*. There are 100,000 times more individuals of this shrimp than humans, and together they weigh about twice as much as all of humanity.

We are advised not to take a competitive stance. Mankind, not the Antarctic shrimp, is liable to destroy the Earth. A sustainable society depends on a limited number of humans.

The five- to six-million years that have passed since we split with the chimpanzees are only a flash in the history of evolution. Consequently we are not that different, biologically speaking. In fact, genetically we are close to 99% identical to chimps. Moreover, genetically we are one of the most homogeneous species of animals, because the 100,000 years that have elapsed since the current populations began to diverge is a short period of time in the evolution of a large mammal. True, the various human populations have been given slightly different external characteristics, such as skin color and facial features; but the variety of lifestyles and thinking that one observes when traveling around the globe are due primarily to cultural differentiation. Individuals may differ in genetic terms, but most of the genetic variants are present in all major populations.

The above observation also implies that we are, genetically, pretty much the same today as were 100,000 years ago. In other

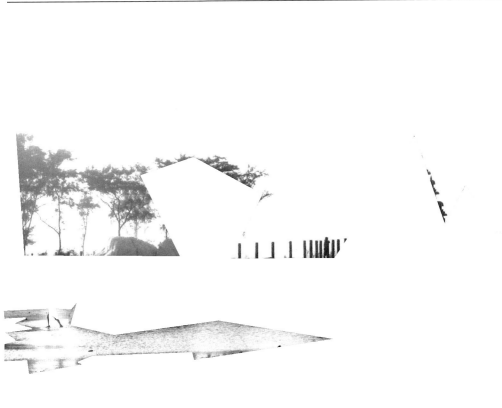

Ancient Hindu temples by the sea, in Mamallapuram, India.

words, present-day humans have the innate propensities of Stone Age man. Yet, neither chimpanzees nor the Stone Ager made any drastic marks on Planet Earth. And they did not understand what the Universe is about, or how it is governed by the laws of physics. Something strange happened over the last ten thousand years, and particularly during the last century! Now we understand. We know roughly what we are, and we have found out how to exploit both nature and physical resources to our own benefit. We may not be almighty, but suddenly we come pretty close, and we do not shy away from using our competence.

This last twist of events could not easily be predicted based on our evolutionary history. Our particular human set of genes has been around for 200,000 years; yet, only recently did things start to happen. It is indeed strange that so much insight, and so much power, have been bestowed upon us.

———

The process of evolution had its quantum leaps, and so too has the progress of human culture. The most significant leap arguably came when we invented agriculture. This actually happened independently in several places at about the same time: in the Middle East, in China, in both Central and South America, and in an area of Africa south of the Sahara. In the period between 10,000 and 7,000 years ago, agriculture-based societies turned up in all these places.[39]

Present-day farming means that a small percentage of the population provides sufficient food to feed more or less everyone. Early farming was drastically different. In those days, growing your own crops was a tough job. People were probably better off as hunters and gatherers, as that life style implied more free time. In fact, the available evidence suggests that humans had better health and longer life expectancy prior to the invention of agriculture. So why tilt the earth and raise your own animals when nature can do the job for you?

The more likely answer is that farming was necessary as a consequence of two factors: increased population density and climatic changes that entailed less naturally occurring food. In short, it became difficult to fill the stomach by hunting and gathering alone.

Early farming meant a lot of toil, but it marked the beginning of a transformation of humanity—for good and bad. Cultivation facilitated the development of large-scale societies simply because it allowed more people to live in a small area. The increase in population density, and the fact that eventually not everybody needed to be involved in obtaining food, opened the way for a crucial innovation: the division of labor. While some individuals cultivated the land, others could concentrate on making clothes and equipment, or exploring Divinity. Without these kinds of larger societies, we would never have reached our present state of science and technology.

As in the case of farming, the formation of advanced nations led by an elite, as well as the development of art and science, also hap-

———

[39] S. Mithen, *After the Ice: A Global Human History 20,000–5,000 BC* (2006).

pened independently in several parts of the world. It seems as if this sort of progress was a predestined consequence of the increase in community size. In other words, farming put in motion a series of events that eventually led to where we stand today. It is possible that climatic changes were instrumental in starting this process, but one may ask whether there were other intervening agents behind the climatic change? Did a Divine Force help the birth of large societies and subsequent civilization?

Whatever caused the initial events, technology has improved continuously ever since. The industrial revolution toward the end of the 18th century represents one of the more recent leaps. Machines started to take on many of the tasks required for sustenance, freeing time for exploration and other enterprises. The latest and arguably most dramatic revolution started in the late 20th century with the development of computers and biotechnology. Today, anybody who can afford a computer can communicate with the rest of the world, and at the same time, without that many keystrokes, gain access to more or less the combined knowledge of mankind. Biotechnology, on the other hand, allows us to interfere with the process of evolution.

The story of mankind is incredible, and possibly it has just begun. If we are the product of some Divine entity, I hope that entity knew what it was doing. If our existence is mere coincidence, I hope *we* know what we are doing.

A Creative Force

Was everything that I have described in this chapter—from the creation of a cosmos to the exploits of mankind—inevitable consequences of the physical laws of the Universe? And if so, were these laws based on coincidences?

When realizing what is required in order to generate a Universe and provide it with intelligent life, the postulate of some primary entity does not appear that weird: The world is too fantastic to be just a fluke. True, chance may very well be involved in what happens here, but it is unlikely to explain why we have a Universe, particularly one that allows destiny to materialize. Random events seem rather to be an instrument used to allow reality to advance.

We try hard to understand how the physical laws could have led to what we have today. Science finds explanations—partly because we insist that there are scientific explanations, even in cases where it may not be within the scope of science to offer a complete elucidation. And even if, as I believe, the sciences got most of it right, it does not make what has happened less astonishing, nor does it make reality less overwhelming. The Universe is still an extraordinary miracle, and there is still room for a creative Force to stand behind it.

Certain events appear to be simply beyond scientific explanations, such as the birth of the Universe and the beginning of life on Earth. Several other occurrences are utterly strange, although not

The cross on top of the hill, Matera, Italy.

completely beyond our attempts at offering explanations. For example, there is the property of carbon and its peculiar production in stars as well as surprising twists in the evolution of life on Earth, including photosynthesis and multicellular organisms.

If one prefers, anything can be ascribed to fortune or fate. And if one happens to appreciate the current situation, call it luck. There is nothing wrong with this way of thinking, but at the same time it might be that one is closing one's eyes to some aspects of reality that are actually worth focusing on. Many people feel that by opting for a more open point of view, a broader vision arises: They recognize the vague contour of a causal and governing entity. It is my belief that we humans have little to lose, but much to gain, by directing our senses toward this Divine entity—a Force somehow outside the purely scientific field of vision.

History is on our side. At some point our ancestors developed the capacity to experience the spiritual aspects of the world, and faith has been with us ever since. Remnants of graves have been found suggesting that not just modern humans, but even the Neandertals, buried their dead with flowers and other objects some 100,000 years ago—a discovery that suggests they practiced religious rituals.[40] More recently—40,000 to 50,000 years ago—modern man developed a culture in which they drew cave paintings and made carved figures; we assume that these objects, too, had religious significance. Then, some 10,000 years ago, humans began to make large constructions in stone. The first objects they made were temple-like structures such as Stonehenge.[41]

Within the course of written history, the amount of money and resources spent on religious activity is overwhelming. Add to that all the time spent worshiping. The evidence suggests that the main focus of human creative activity has been directed toward the Divine. We do not quite know when it started, but at some point, we found God; or, if you prefer, God appeared for us.

---

[40] R. A. Solecki, "Shanidar IV, a Neanderthal Flower Burial in Northern Iraq," *Science* 190 (1975): 880–81; or R. Lewin, *Human Evolution: An Illustrated Introduction* (1999).
[41] A. Curry, "Seeking the Roots of Ritual," *New Scientist* (January 18, 2008): 278–80.

Deserted church in the Pyrenees, France.

CHAPTER FOUR

A stone circle in use by the spiritual village of Tamera, Portugal.

To Be Human

Divine Directives

Most creeds are concerned with the following two issues: One is to explain the various phenomena people wonder about in their daily lives, including how the world was created. The second main issue involves advice for living—not only how to improve your personal quality of life but also how you ought to relate to your fellow human beings. Religious guidance includes the subject of morality, but it is also intended to help people in personal activities. In a way, the counseling aspect of religion is more important than the issue of understanding the environment; after all, quality of life and the well-being of society matter more. As in the case of the Story of Creation, most religious recommendations were formulated in an era long ago. Since then, human wisdom has expanded and the conditions of living have changed.

In the previous chapter, I offered an update of the two aspects listed above by discussing where science stands today in relation to them. The majority of people may agree that science is crucial for understanding the Universe. However, the contribution of science in formulating rules of ethics is perhaps more controversial. True, science may not be in a position to offer highly specific or exact guidance; yet, in my mind several fields of science, including medicine, the social sciences, and biologically based knowledge on the nature of being human are relevant for the pursuit of devising sensible advice. Science offers a perspective that any culture, including the cultures associated with the various faiths, should keep in mind when handling ethical issues. I am confident that the writers of religious texts did their best to incorporate the wisdom available at the time. There is, however, cause to take a critical look at some of the ancient ideas that are still influential today in the light of present knowledge. The purpose of the present chapter is to introduce some topics that future creeds may find relevant when evaluating their principles.

———

In order to find our way, we first need to know where we want to go. In the case of society, it is essential to set up priorities. An individual ought to consider how one wants to spend a lifetime. The overriding objective for both these endeavors may be defined as optimizing quality of life. This appears to be a reasonably neutral intent that most people may subscribe to. The quest does, however, get a bit more complicated when one tries to define what "quality of life" is actually about. I shall present an answer to this challenge—an answer based on a biological view of human nature.

Biology paints a broad picture of mankind, while the social sciences add details. That is, while the natural sciences offer an account of the human species, the social sciences are better at describing individual and cultural differences. Biology educates us about how evolution has shaped our genes, and thus what innate dispositions and behavioral tendencies the average human is born with. For me, this perspective points toward certain suggestions about what constitutes a good life and how society may be organized with quality of life as an ultimate aim. There are several alternative approaches to the issue of guidance, including those based on other traditions, but they tend to be tuned toward particular societies or cultures. The biological perspective offers a common ground, particularly since the human species is rather homogeneous, genetically speaking.

In the ensuing section of this chapter I shall take a closer look at Quality of Life. There is a rich and varied literature offering readers all sorts of directions supposedly leading toward bliss; the present discussion, however, is restricted to a biological interpretation of happiness and offers concomitant counsel.[1]

The third section suggests a related, science-based background for a discussion of ethics: Morality.

Religion also has considerable potential to influence people in questions related to happiness and morality. In order to exploit this potential, it is essential to develop the ability to sense God. The

---

[1] Besides the text directing people toward a religiously based salvation, there are a number of books detailing an approach based on social sciences. The following treatises are recommended: D. G. Myers, *Pursuit of Happiness* (1993); M. Seligman, *Authentic Happiness* (2004); S. Klein and S. Lehmann, *The Science of Happiness* (2006); and E. Diener and R. Biswas-Diener, *Happiness: Unlocking the Mysteries of Psychological Wealth* (2008).

fourth and final section therefore considers how to search for—and engage in—Divinity, i.e., "Listening to God's Whisper" p. 159.

The purpose of this book is neither to create a new religion, nor to revolutionize the moral views of society. The rationale for this chapter rests with the idea that "knowing thyself" is useful, and that insight into human nature may point toward minor changes with regard to ways of thinking and living. Most of the recommendations that have emerged in the context of traditional faith systems have merit, but in some cases modifications may be in order. This does not require any depreciation of the fundamental religious doctrines, but simply to acknowledge that the present situation is different. Today we have more relevant knowledge, knowledge that was unavailable in ancient times; moreover, the circumstances have changed in ways that ought to impact the advice offered.

As a hypothetical thought, what if everyone agreed on how life ought to be lived—for example, to put the focus on health, happiness, and compassion—and that we knew how to get there? The challenge then would be to convince people to follow such advice. Divine doctrines have a certain potential for influencing people's behavior when compared to secular laws or scientific reasoning in that those who sense God tend to enjoy adapting to Divine recommendations. For those religiously inclined, following such advice is not only voluntary, but also associated with positive feelings. True, most churches have coercive strategies within their repertoire—e.g., threatening with a life in hell—but these strategies are aimed primarily at the less devoted adherents. The point here being that God may help us bring forth useful guidance with a minimal use of coercion.

The religious approach is probably at its best when offering recommendations rather than commandments. If a rule of conduct is important, but not adhered to voluntarily, then secular laws with concomitant punishment may be a more useful strategy. In other words, it seems more constructive for the priest to offer a reward—for example, eternal life in the heaven of one's choice—rather than threaten someone with everlasting hell. Most people do not mind well-intended counsel, but they dislike intimidating rules that are not sensed as meaningful. For those who have faith, the Word of God has the significance required to be consequential.

The primary task, in my mind, is to obtain the best background possible for evaluating what the advice, religious or not, ought to be. The following sections are meant as an attempt to point out relevant information.

Quality of Life

What is happiness? Philosophers have asked this question for millennia, while scientists have only recently started to take an interest. Traditionally, misery has been the primary concern for psychologists, but under headings such as *positive psychology* and *subjective well-being* many of them are now also trying to tackle the better side of life.

I take a different approach to the question of happiness. As a starting point I look at why evolution has shaped us with the capacity for feelings of good or bad experiences. Feelings are produced by the brain; happiness (and sadness) depend on the fact that this lump of nervous tissue was bestowed on us by Evolution. You may enjoy the sight of a flower, and if the flower is in a good spot with ample water, it has every reason to rejoice. The point is that it does not rejoice. A flower cannot experience either sorrow or joy simply because it lacks the structures required for having feelings. Similarly, a simple neurological system, such as that of an earthworm, may not fulfill the requirements for the word "happiness" to carry much meaning. The nervous system of the earthworm is presumably designed for pure reflexes without any deliberation.

The primary purpose of feelings is to help the brain make decisions; behavior based on reflexes does not require that sort of help. In other words, a more advanced brain is required, preferably one with the capacity to recognize a preferred state of mind. The mammalian brain qualifies, and the increased dependence on conscious experiences in the human lineage makes the distinction between good or bad particularly pertinent. Thus, the capacity to enjoy life is a consequence of our evolutionary history. In fact, we may be the one species with the greatest capacity for happiness; unfortunately, it also comes with a concomitant capacity for sorrow.

A Tamil wedding taking place in Norway.

I have previously written extensively on the evolutionary approach to understanding happiness, using the term *Darwinian Happiness*; here I shall only offer a brief description of the main principles.[2]

---

[2] The more extensive treatise can be found in B. Grinde, *Darwinian Happiness: Evolution as a Guide for Living and Understanding Human Behavior* (The Darwin Press, Inc., 2002); shorter, but more scientific accounts, in B. Grinde, "Happiness in the Perspective of Evolutionary Psychology," *Journal of Happiness Studies* 3 (2002): 331–54; or B. Grinde, "Darwinian Happiness: Can the Evolutionary Perspective on Well-being Help Us Improve Society?" *World Futures—The Journal of General Evolution* 60 (2004): 317–29.

Quality of life is intrinsically linked with three aspects of how the human brain is designed by the process of evolution. I shall first summarize the relevant features, and then delve a little further into each.

I. A main function of the brain is to offer positive and negative feelings aimed at directing behavior.[3]

II. The combination of intellect and self-consciousness is important; it allows us to recognize our feelings and assess which experiences are to be appreciated.

III. There is presumably a default state of contentment, which is the preferred state of mind as long as nothing is bothering us. Disease, hunger, stress, and anxiety are examples of conditions that tend to ruin the default contentment.

I.   The first of the three features important for our quality of life concerns the capacity to differentiate between positive and negative feelings or sensations. The main function of the brain is to care for the interest of the genes by orchestrating behavior. The primary focus is to sense the environment, evaluate options, and act accordingly. Sensations and other forms of feelings are generated to help us make the right choice; more specifically, the brain is designed to offer two broad types of instigations: First, it directs us *toward* behavior considered appropriate for the genes, such as eating and having sex; and, second, it directs us *away* from behavior deemed damaging, such as burning a finger or breaking a leg. These two opposite types of instigations are, for good reasons, coupled with opposite types of commotions—respectively, pleasant and unpleasant feelings. The former may be referred to as "brain rewards," and the latter as "brain punishment." The obvious idea is that the individual should learn by experience how to avoid pain, and how to find and engage in agreeable stimuli.

The best interests of the genes were in focus during the evolution of the human brain, but this does not mean we need to abide by whatever our genes might "wish." Biologically, success is measured by the number of offspring; thus, procreation is closest to the

---

[3] For a detailed, scientific review of the neurological mechanisms behind positive and negative experiences, see S. Leknes and I. Tracey, "A Common Neurobiology for Pain and Pleasure," *Nature Review of Neuroscience* 9 (2008): 314–20.

heart of our genes. Yet, although children can be a great source of delight, our quality of life does not depend on them (and for some parents may in fact be lessened by them). Moreover, eating sweets was adaptive behavior in the Stone Age because sweet treats were rare; today it may cause obesity and diabetes. In other words, what the genes are designed to consider sensible behavior is not necessarily what is best for us.

The brain offers the opportunity to enjoy our actions even if they are inappropriate for the purpose of breeding. An obvious example concerns our capacity to enjoy sex in the presence of contraceptives. As contraceptives were not known during the formative period of human evolution, the brain gladly dishes out the same rewards, whether the act has the potential to lead to impregnation or not.

All vertebrates, and very likely some invertebrates as well, are able to sense pain and pleasure. What happened in the evolutionary branch leading toward us was that these feelings became more conscious. Instead of responding instinctively, we can reflect on the value of various experiences and, based on that, decide what to do next. In other words, we were given a generous portion of *free will*.

Actually, as a consequence of our free will, we may be the species with the most potent brain rewards and punishments. The more power of decision that rests with conscious contemplation, the more reasons the genes have for installing powerful instigations. There is indeed evidence suggesting an increased expression of endorphins (a central component of brain rewards) in humans compared to other mammals.[4]

All pleasures are not necessarily equally pleasurable, and all pain is not equally hard to bear. We sometimes torment ourselves for the purpose of later advantages—when, for instance, accepting an unpleasant, but well paid, job. At other times we resist satisfaction due to the adverse long-term consequences, such as when deciding not to eat that piece of cake. Optimal exploitation of the brain's potential for positive and negative experiences obviously demands a life-long perspective.

We tend to be pretty sure about what we want. That, however, does not imply that we make sensible decisions. The brain's reper-

---

[4] M. Balter, "Expression of Endorphin Gene Favored in Human Evolution," *Science* 310 (2005): 1257.

toire of feelings is designed for Stone Age conditions, which are not always suitable for present conditions. In those days there were no pubs or shops offering whatever suits our taste. Industry has caught up with the human reward system and eagerly sells all sorts of products designed to push the reward buttons. Consequently, it is easy to find means to exploit the reward system, but also more difficult to avoid the various traps of misuse. Narcotics are probably the most obvious and most dangerous trap, but there are plenty of other dubious opportunities, from fatty food to gambling.

The notion that we face pleasure and pain seems obvious, but are really all experiences either good or bad? The immediate answer may be "no," because most of the time life passes by as a smooth and neutral stream. However, if we take a close look at our experiences—that is, whatever ripples that may occur in that stream—and if we allow for a certain semantic flexibility, you may agree that most ripples can be categorized as either ups or downs. Moreover, our general mood may range from depressed to high spirited.

A reasonable strategy toward enhanced happiness may be to become more aware of the minor rewards associated with everyday life. Take a closer look at the trees or flowers we pass by on our way to work and engage in the sensations evoked. Or take the trouble of smiling at people you meet and savor the smiles they return. Part of the art of living is to exploit the possibilities for pleasures that we all have, and that do not need to be bought. In short, we ought to learn to absorb the simple joys of life.

Knowledge about what sort of triggers are available for, respectively, rewards or punishment is relevant because insight into these aspects of the brain can help us make rational decisions. (In *The Sensible Hedonist*, below, I take a closer look at the topic.)

The Sensible Hedonist

It is not easy to achieve an optimal life quality. For one thing, the inherent tendency toward self-indulgence and earthly pleasures complicates the situation. Hedonism is a rewarding yet treacherous path in a world where all forms of pleasures are available in superfluous doses simply by opening your purse—optimized, of course, for your indulgence by the forces of market economics.

The pitfalls are obvious. Even if we manage to stay clear of the more dangerous stimuli capable of triggering brain rewards, such as psychoactive drugs ranging from heroin to alcohol, we may easily ruin our long-term health, or at least our teeth, by eating candy and drinking cola. The potential rewards of exercising are easily lost in the pleasures of a deep sofa in front of a TV. The simple satisfaction offered by our capacity for default contentment tends to drown in the soup of pleasure. Our innate tendencies help us understand the pitfalls of a modern life style: In the Stone Age, temptations suited to stimulate brain rewards were rare and exploited when available, as otherwise the opportunity would likely vanish. Today there are too many opportunities, and exploiting them is ruining our health.

As a rule of thumb any appropriate use of body and mind is coupled with rewarding sensations for those who manage to tune in. In other words, the brain offers incentives for us to act according to what the genes have programmed our minds to consider beneficial. Thus, positive experiences can be harvested by a vast assortment of behaviors, including using the toilet or running a marathon. But we may need a bit of training in order to focus on, and thus fully sense, the subtle rewards. The point being that the hedonism option does not require that we ruin our health.

In fact, even situations that have a distinct negative attribute, such as grief, may offer a positive experience. Grief is a reaction that evolved to help us handle certain types of events, such as the loss of a spouse. In a way, it implies a sort of punishing reaction, because our genes are best served if we avoid losing our mate, but it is also a useful reaction to the situation we are in: A display of sorrow or low mood may illicit support from others, and as such it is a state of mind the genes encourage. When the genes encourage something, they tend to do so by coupling it with a reward. Consequently, sorrow may feel "good," although the feeling is obviously quite different from the pleasure of eating ice cream. This point may help explain why people enjoy movies that make them cry: Films offer the opportunity of harvesting the rewards of grief without suffering any personal loss.

Two individuals can experience the same situation in a rather different way. Some people love the excitement of imminent danger, while others are just scared stiff. The joys of a challenge are due to what is referred to as an adrenalin kick. Our bodies produce adrenalin in times of danger in order to prepare us to do our best.

Sometimes it is in our genes' interest that we defy, or even seek, danger—for example, when hunting big game. Thus the adrenalin is coupled with rewards; however, in order to enjoy them, we need to feel on top of the situation. Rock climbing can be exhilarating, but if the climber slips and falls, the excitement may be replaced by unpleasant fright, injury, or death.

It makes sense to improve quality of life by exploiting the reward system, but in order to have long-term success, one needs to choose the triggers carefully. Possibly the most profitable option is to focus the mind on positive aspects of everyday living. Lots of stimuli can elicit rewards, but unless one takes the time to delve into or deal with the sensations, they do not add much to one's happiness. Prudent doses of cakes and wine may add to one's lifetime score, but walking in the forest or touching God may serve us even better.

II. The second feature, the combination of intellect and self-consciousness, implies that we have the capacity to care about how we are doing. Happiness matters and we are able to make conscious efforts toward improving the situation. Science has recently begun to understand why we have this feature, what parts of the brain are involved, and how awareness is regulated.[5]

Actually you do not know much about what your brain, or for that matter the rest of your body, is up to. Most of what takes place in your head is withheld from the conscious parts of the brain. You have no idea how your liver is functioning, and you do not recognize the signals passing between the nervous system and the intestines to regulate the peristaltic activity that pushes the food downwards. Consciousness is a feature designed for a particular purpose: It makes the individual capable of regulating behavior in a more flexible manner than what pure instincts would allow, which is to say it makes you better prepared to respond to novel challenges and unexpected events. Consciousness, however, is set up to engage in only select types of challenges.

---

[5] S. Laurey, "Eyes Open, Brain Shut," *Scientific American* (May 2007): 66–71; and J. A. Hobson, "REM Sleep and Dreaming: Towards a Theory of Protoconsciousness," *Nature Reviews Neuroscience* 10 (2009): 803–13.

The point is that by letting the higher functions of the brain contemplate possible actions, which implies taking into account previous experience, you are likely to come up with more optimal solutions. Reflexes and instinctive behavior are not quite up to the task. For example, in order to hunt down a prey it helps to have detailed knowledge and experience about the species you are chasing; you need to be able to follow the tracks of the animal, conceive a useful strategy for the kill, and be trained in the use of weapons. In humans these elements are an intrinsic part of our intellect, making us the most dangerous predator on the face of the Earth.

Although the brain has a grip on much of what goes on in your body, you—by which I mean your conscious self—are only allowed to engage in a minor part of it. The remainder—i.e., what evolution has considered it best for you not to know—is thus cared for by brain modules outside the scope of attention. As they say in business, "Information is given on a need to know basis only." You are not, for example, allowed to interfere with your heart—for what if, in a moment of despair, you decided to stop the beat? It certainly would not be in the interest of your genes. Similarly, although you may choose to hold your breath until you faint, at that point the autonomic nervous system will again take control and cause you to start breathing. Your genes do not allow you to die that easily.

Awareness may be restricted to a fraction of what goes on in body and brain, but that fraction includes the features that matter. It embraces the parts that add meaning and quality to your life and defines what you are. All your emotions and feelings are, by definition, included in your awareness. However, you should know that much of the input controlling your sensations actually stems from subconscious parts of the brain. (See Appendix V: *Be Conscious of Your Subconscious*, p. 203, for a further discussion.)

———

Many people claim that the most important issue regarding quality of life is to find a meaning in life. It is not obvious why this should be so important, but one factor that may help explain this sentiment is the contentment associated with having a purpose. This form of satisfaction has to do with an innate feature of the brain that says, "Do something useful."

As our consciousness and free will expanded, it became important for the genes to install that sort of disposition in order to avoid ending up in an overly lazy body. Presumably it helped "survival" to stimulate the individual toward being dynamic, as most activities would be devoted to obtaining resources, caring for offspring, or socializing. At the very least, doing something would tend to be a learning experience. Obviously, the pursuits available during the formative period of human evolution were limited; collecting stamps or playing computer games were not an option. Today there is an endless list of activities we can engage in while sending the following message to our brains: "At least I am doing something." Finding a meaning in life is thus a question of activating a certain form of brain reward, but this particular reward is closely associated with the development of consciousness in the human lineage.

The rewards associated with being useful may be exploited. There are, however, reasons to reflect on which activities you ought to engage in. Whether or not your choices actually help your genes is of limited concern; what matters more is to what extent they really present a long-term benefit to your quality of life. Collecting stamps may serve you well, but engaging in voluntary social work may serve you even better. For the sake of your community, the latter suggestion has obvious advantages. Moreover, kindness engages another reward module as well: Acts of compassion are coupled with a definite potential for gratification.

Today, money appears to be the main substitute for utility value. We simply try to "make money." Installing wealth as the main purpose in life is a two-edged sword: On the one hand, the economy is an essential ingredient in developing the niceties of industrialized society; on the other hand, the associated greed does not always serve either individual or society well.

Most cultures encourage the "be useful" sentiment; after all, this predisposition tends to help both the community and the individual in his or her pursuit of happiness. The cultural promotion further explains why utility and meaning so often are mentioned when people are asked about what matters in life.

———

III. The third important aspect of the brain concerns the presumed default *state of contentment.* Psychologists have long known that most people are overly optimistic. We tend to believe that our chances of success are better than they really are, a propensity that nurtures gambling, but that also keeps us cheerful and helps us retain a positive attitude to life. The point here being that, as long as the basic requirements of health, survival, and sustenance are met, the brain tends to retain an encouraging attitude.

The above statement is based on empirical findings. For example, when asked how we feel compared to an average person, the majority responds that they are most certainly happier than the average. The statement, however, also fits with a theoretical perspective: It ought to be in the genes' interest to reside in a person with a "let's push ahead" attitude to life. Such a person is more likely to face challenges and to find the energy required for tasks ahead. In other words, a vital and happy optimist has a better chance of success in obtaining food or a mate compared to a depressed pessimist. Thus, as long as there is no particular reason to lose your spirit, the brain should give you a good time. We are born to be happy—or at least content.

That, however, does not imply that people *are* happy. The problem of our present society is that things are not always as they should be; consequently the default contentment is easily lost. Even if basic sustenance is assured, stress and psychological problems tend to rob us of joy. As revealed by the statistics of health, material wealth has not been able to shield us from mental diseases. During any given year, about one-fourth of the population of the United States is in need of psychological support, the more common problems being associated with anxiety, depression, and sleep. Moreover, patients seeking medical attention probably only account for the tip of the iceberg when assessing the actual impact mental problems have on the quality of life. Many people have lost their joy of life without necessarily qualifying for any diagnosable mental disorder.[6]

A broken arm or an amputated leg does not need to trigger more than short-term fluctuations in happiness. Even after accidents that cause people to be considerably handicapped, most people, it seems, would return to the pre-accident level of joy within a reasonably short time. However, as the capacity for good feelings rests

---

[6] See C. J. L. Murray and A. D. Lopez, *The Global Burden of Disease: A Comprehensive Assessment of Mortality and Disability from Diseases, Injuries and Risk Factors in 1990 and Projected to 2020* (1996); or *Mental Health—A Report of the Surgeon General* (National Institute of Mental Health, 1999).

with the brain, it is more difficult to retain the good mood when the brain itself is the problem.

It seems unlikely that the present prevalence of mental diseases reflects the normal situation for the human species. During the Stone Age, people with those sorts of problems would presumably have serious difficulties with regard to surviving and procreating. Selection tends to remove genes that could lead to any form of incapacitating disease or condition, including those affecting the mind; thus, a reasonable conclusion is that the high prevalence of mental problems reflects particular attributes of the present way of life—that is, we are talking about diseases of civilization. Apparently some features of the modern environment tend to impair our minds, and thus our capacity for contentment.

You still find the smile and twinkle in the eyes of children—whether they are rich or poor. The smiles, however, tend to wither with age—at least in industrialized societies. My impression from visiting tribal people in Africa and Asia is that the radiance of joy lasts longer there. It seems as if more individuals retain their default contentment in the tribal setting, at least in those places where they have suitable conditions of life and the pressure from the industrialized world does not eradicate traditional sentiments. It is also my impression that a similar form of contentment can be observed in animals. The question then is: What can a citizen of a Western city do in order to retain natural contentment?

The concepts of *flow* and *mindfulness*, and the practices associated with these theories, offer a bit of an answer. In my mind these concepts are closely related to what I refer to as default contentment. (For a discussion, see *Let It Flow*, below).

Let It Flow

It is possible to feel satisfaction without engaging the more overt pleasure functions of the brain. A range of philosophers and psychologists has made the point, albeit using a variety of phrases. Altogether, the various descriptions revolve around the issue of harmony within, along with the absence of stress. Or, in the context of meditation, the desired state of affairs may be referred to as inner peace and a balanced mind.

The psychologist Mihaly Csikszentmihalyi uses the word "flow" for the feeling evoked by immersing oneself in a task. The way he sees it, the idea is to be present with the full force of awareness in whatever activity is at hand, whether washing dishes or making love; and that by doing so we harvest the associated rewards.[7]

"Mindfulness" is a related concept. It is about focusing on our self. We are human beings and should relate to what is happening inside the mind. It is a question of taking on daily routines with the kind of focus needed when balancing on a tight rope. In a way, the intention is to enter a meditative state while going on with daily chores.

For me, all these depictions of a good life are related to the present concept of default contentment, perhaps with the added feature of "meaning of life." Evolution has shaped humans, and other mammals, to delight in life unless circumstances dictate something else. The art of living is to avoid losing this predisposition to stress or mental imbalance.

There is hope even for those who are not quite there. It is possible to train the brain—for example, by employing meditative techniques. It is, however, also possible to "appeal to" God for help. Engaging in religion offers a pathway to positive experiences, whether referred to as bliss, flow, or contentment. Monastic life typically revolves around finding this sort of satisfaction, whether one is engaging in prayer or growing vegetables. As a human behavioral biologist, I would say that work was never meant to be a burden, simply because caring for life's necessities is in line with the desire of the genes and is thus associated with potential pleasures. Some people tend to consider work as an undesirable obligation, although for many people it is in fact unnecessary (in that they have the means to survive without), but desirable. A job may not be required for contentment, but approached with the right mind, work can be a valuable tool in the quest for happiness. So, whatever you are up to, let it flow.

There is, however, another way of looking at the problem. When people first started to bring in wild animals and display them in zoological gardens, the attitude was that, as long as the animals were fed and offered a decent shelter, they ought to be happy. But the animals were quite obviously unhappy. They wandered restlessly

[7] M. Csikszentmihalyi, *Finding Flow: The Psychology of Engagement with Everyday Life* (1998).

back and forth in the cage, scraped themselves bloody against the walls, and refused to eat. Eventually the zookeepers realized that in order to make them thrive, it was not sufficient to offer food; the animals also required an environment as close as possible to the environment evolution had shaped them to live in. Baboons, for example, are social animals and should therefore belong to a group, while orangutans are adapted to a more solitary way of life. A zoo can never offer the perfect conditions for wild beasts, but it is possible to modify and improve the enclosures substantially.

Modern society appears to have certain similarities with a suboptimal zoo, in that the environment is rather different from the Stone Age type of environment for which evolution has shaped us. I believe that this difference helps explain not just the typical somatic diseases of civilization, such as obesity and heart disease, but also the high prevalence of mental disorders, such as anxiety and depression. Moreover, it may explain why people apparently tend to lose their joy of life. In other words, it seems as if present zookeepers are doing a better job with animals than our politicians are doing with humans.[8]

I do not suggest that we should return to the Stone Age; science and industry have so much to offer. It is possible to improve the conditions for zoo animals within the restrictions imposed by captivity; in a similar way it should be possible to adjust certain aspects of society within the restrictions of an industrialized country. We should try to retain the advantages of modern medicine and technology, but at the same time create an environment more in tune with the nature of being human.

There are numerous differences, or mismatches as they are typically referred to, between the present way of life and that of our ancestors. Some of them are what I refer to as *discords,* which means that they cause an increased vulnerability to afflictions or a suboptimal quality of life.

All bodily functions are potentially vulnerable to discords; for example, many people suffer from pain in muscles and joints due to unnatural work situations, such as sitting all day long in front of a

---

[8] For more on these thoughts, see D. Morris, *The Human Zoo* (1966); B. Grinde, *Darwinian Happiness* (2002); or B. Grinde, "Can the Concept of Discords Help Us Find the Causes of Mental Diseases?" *Medical Hypothesis* 73 (2009): 106–9.

computer. Yet our brain is probably the most vulnerable organ. It constitutes, arguably, the most complex part of our bodies, and it is designed to develop in intimate interaction with the environment. If the environment is different from what the genes "expect," development is easily distorted. For example, the high prevalence of anxiety-related problems may reflect excessive stimulation of the fear function, particularly at the time of infancy, the consequence being that the fear module turns out to be more dominant than if it had developed in a natural setting.[9]

In a child who never gets the chance to move around, muscles will atrophy, and even if the individual compensates by starting training later in life, it is difficult to obtain optimal muscle strength. In the same way it is possible to take therapy, or in other ways try to compensate for quandaries concerning the brain, but it seems to be even more difficult to amend adverse features of the mind. Apparently the brain modules involved in happiness and contentment are among the more vulnerable with regard to discords; thus, if the brain is a victim of unfavorable conditions, it is less likely to serve you well in the sense of offering you a good life. Moreover, if your knees or your arm muscles are in bad shape, you may still obtain a high score as to quality of life; but if the problem rests with your state of mind, the score tends to drop drastically. Anxiety and depression, for example, hit hard on happiness.

The way defensive functions of the mind are designed also contributes to the loss of pleasure. The main forms of defense—fear and low mood—are involved in security and in avoiding assault. Hyperactivity of the fear response may lead to anxiety disorders, while too much activity of the low-mood response may cause depression. Both fear and low-mood can be regarded as punishing sensations designed to help avoid situations that cause their activation. For example, one learns to avoid moving to the edge of a cliff where one risks falling down. The problem with these responses is two-fold: One, they are designed to be easily triggered, because failure to activate fear in a threatening situation can cause a lot more damage than excessive activation; and two, even a minor hyperactivity of these responses tends to have a drastic impact on quality of life.

---

[9] B. Grinde, "An Approach to the Prevention of Anxiety-Related Disorders Based on Evolutionary Medicine," *Preventive Medicine* 40 (2005): 904–9.

The rule of thumb emanating from the above discussion is that we should try to adjust our way of life according to the sort of conditions evolution has shaped us to live under. Obviously this is a rule with many exceptions: Most people prefer to take antibiotics rather than die (in a natural way) from bacterial infections, and sleeping on a mattress is better for your health compared to sleeping on muddy ground. It is, in other words, important to distinguish between mismatches and discords. The latter are the ones we should worry about as they imply a kind of stress in regard to physical or mental health.

Discords are, by definition, potentially harmful. Yet, for some people a particular discord may not matter, while others are vulnerable. Certain individuals may tap on a keyboard all day long without developing any aches, while others feel the pain at the sheer sight of a computer.

I believe the most problematic discords in our present society are those related to social life. We were meant to live in a tribal setting where there are life-long ties and commitments within a small group of people. Today what is left is, at best, a nuclear family and a handful of acquaintances that one occasionally meets. At the same time there is a constant flux of more or less friendly strangers that require attention in the shop, while driving to work, or just walking the streets. For many people the social network is fragile and lasting commitments are rare. Common consequences of this discord presumably include loneliness and depression.

Individualism has a strong position in our society. Unfortunately, the concomitant desire for independence may function somewhat like a narcotic: We want our personal freedom, but fail to see the costs. There are obvious advantages of doing whatever we want, whenever we want it, without having to consider other people, but the long-term consequences may be isolation and lack of a social network. Humans are shaped to be a highly gregarious species. Our quality of life is likely to improve by giving up part of our freedom for the sake of investing more in communal connections.[10]

---

[10] B. Grinde, "An Evolutionary Perspective on the Importance of Social Relations for Quality of Life," *The Scientific World Journal* 9 (2009): 588–605.

Can God help us improve quality of life? I believe the answer is "yes" and offer six arguments as to why we may benefit from religion:

1. We have evolved the capacity to sense a Divine presence and this sensation is linked with brain rewards. For many people, relating to God offers the optimal in bliss. Nursing this aspect of human nature is a sensible strategy for gaining happiness.

2. God offers companionship. People tend to be lonely even in the midst of the densest crowds. Being in touch with God may substitute for the social connections they lack, as it is common for believers to feel intimately related with God.

3. People congregate in churches and temples for communal worship; thus, religion promotes real social life as well. The social network of the parishioners is usually strong, inasmuch as members meet regularly and have shared interests and values.

4. Religion offers hope and consolation. Faith may reduce anxiety by giving a sense of a protective agent, and by suggesting a life after death.

5. Religion contributes toward a meaning of life: We exist as part of the Creation and are here for the purpose of serving God. Steven Weinberg who was awarded a Nobel Prize in Physics, once lamented that the more comprehensible the Universe became, the more meaningless everything seemed.[11] Granted, we may dislike the idea that we are here on Planet Earth for no purpose, and it is hard to find a purpose amidst a strictly physical view of the cosmos, but the religious perspective suggests an alternative stance: We are here to experience the Creation; we are the eyes and ears that comprehend what the Universe is about. Moreover, we can preside over what is happening—at least in our corner of the world.

6. Religion helps us follow rules that are sensible, but difficult to adhere to. For example, the commandments make it easier to restrain from temptations that have unfortunate long-term consequences: The misuse of alcohol and drugs is less of a threat for those who consider them offensive to God.

---

[11] S. Weinberg, *Facing Up: Science and Its Cultural Adversaries* (2001).

The six issues raised above are not meant to be exhaustive, but they do point toward highly relevant opportunities offered by engaging in religion. Then again, there are also possible negative factors; for example, certain creeds do not encourage, or allow, people to take advantage of the brain's potential for having a good life. Thus, being religious may not serve all of us equally well, but several scientific studies conclude that those who have faith in God are indeed on the average healthier and happier.[12]

For some people it is a paradox that, if God created mankind, why do we have this considerable potential for suffering? Why not give us everlasting joy?

In my mind, humans were created by what may be referred to as a Divine Force, but this Force operated by means of the process of evolution. Evolution has certain limitations: It has to comply with the physical laws of the Universe, which again may depend on various unknown factors. Negative feelings, such as pain and a low mood, were included because they serve vital functions. For example, some people are born with a rare disease (congenital analgesia) that manifests itself as a failure to sense pain. The patients typically die at an early age because they are unable to avoid physical damage to their bodies. Pain is important!

Moreover, in order to let evolution proceed toward more advanced organisms with improved intellectual power, aging and death are required elements. Thus, they too are important. (See *Tools of Evolution: Sex and Death*, p. 104.)

Another relevant point is that the evolutionary process is incapable of creating optimal organisms. That is simply not the way it works. Evolution does bring forth species that survive and procreate, but not necessarily with the best possible properties with regard to either physical functions or quality of life. Living organisms are necessarily fragile, thus illness and injury are to be expected.[13]

---

[12] See, for example, H. G. Koenig and H. J. Cohen, *The Link Between Religion and Health* (2002); or A. L. Ferriss, "Religion and the Quality of Life," *Journal of Happiness Studies* 3 (2002): 199–215.

[13] Evolution is responsible for several "mistakes" in that the solutions chosen are dubious. For a discussion of some examples, see C. Ainsworth and M. L. Page, "Evolution's Greatest Mistakes," *New Scientist* (August 11, 2007): 36–39.

Yet another relevant concern is that evolution depends on competition and conflicts, both within a species and between and among species. As a consequence, we feel anger and indignation toward others, and some of us may take pleasure in meting out malice to the extent that we can enjoy hitting or killing not only animals of prey, but also fellow humans. Other carnivores presumably derive a pleasant sensation from killing us.

The above mentioned features were required for evolution to produce ever more advanced forms of life as well as, finally, our own species. At least it was necessary according to our understanding of what life is about. So, would it have been impossible to bring forth intelligent life without aggression, assertiveness, and suffering?

Trees do not feel any pain, but then again neither do they feel pleasure. Brainpower appears to require an interaction with the environment that includes a variety of experiences; in other words, it is very difficult to imagine an organism with only pleasant sensations. Moreover, the contrast between good and bad is a central element in appreciating what is good. It ought to be preferable to live with pain and worry, rather than have no feelings at all.

The term *peak experience,* as coined by the psychologist Abraham Maslow, is used a lot in connection with the human capacity to enjoy life.[14] Peak experiences are especially joyous and exciting moments in life. The intense feeling of happiness typically comes on suddenly. The experience may have a spiritual dimension—for example, in the sense of an awareness of a greater unity, but it may also be evoked by meditation, love, music, natural scenery, or triggered by psychoactive substances.

For me it is a question of tapping into, or perhaps "super-activating," the brain's potential for initiating rewarding feelings. Presumably, the evolutionary rational for brain rewards is to instigate the type of behavior that release them. Given that we have an innate tendency towards religiousness, it is conceivable that entertaining spiritual experiences are meant to elicit that sort of exhilaration. Most likely all the rewards the brain is set to deliver converge on a shared neurological correlate in the brain. In order to take full advantage of the brain's reward mechanisms, one needs to have a healthy mind; that is, a mind not corrupted by stress but with intact default contentment.

---

[14] A. H. Maslow, *Religions, Values, and Peak-Experiences* (1964).

Evolution has not given us a life devoid of suffering, but we can make the most of the situation. It is within our capacity to derive pleasure and joy from life, and it is possible to nurse and expand these aspects of human nature. And when disease or misfortune hits, it helps to find comfort in God.

Morality

Those who are less familiar with the process of evolution typically assume that nature is the scene of incessant fighting where only the strongest survive. This is not true. The behavioral repertoire of animals includes a lot more than aggression; in fact, survival often depends as much on cooperation as on hostility. Most organisms are involved in extensive, mutually beneficial collaboration with other species, a phenomenon referred to as symbiosis. A considerable number of mammals not only engage in symbiosis, but also in partnership within the species. Humans are an obvious example. Evolution has equipped us with a particularly potent capacity for teamwork, without which societies could not exist. Intelligence by itself is not sufficient to expand science and technology; it all depends on the innate urge to cooperate with others. (See *The Social Sense,* p. 110, for further discussion. See also *Together We Are More,* below.)

Together We Are More

Symbiosis implies that individuals from different species collaborate in a way that benefits both species. It is one of the most beautiful ideas evolution has ever come up with—beautiful because we humans like the idea of collaborating, and beautiful because symbiosis gave rise to the most decorative element in nature: flowers.

Flowers are a consequence of a partnership between plants and animals, the latter being primarily insects, but also some birds. Bees, for example, find nutrients in the flower, while the flower gains by having the bee take care of its sexual activity—an area in which plants generally are not overly adept. The pollen of one flower sticks to the insect, and is subsequently smeared out on the pistil of the next flower.

All species of life depend in some way on one another, yet symbiosis implies a bit more—that two species are of particular importance for each other. It is a special situation, but not uncommon. Actually, most higher forms of life are involved in at least certain types of alliances. For example, the way we handle farm plants can be construed as a sort of symbiosis: They give us food and we give them acres where they can dominate.

We are also partners in a different symbiotic relationship that you may not be aware of. Our closest collaborators are bacteria—some 2,000 difference species of them. They live in our mouths, guts, and skin, most commonly to our advantage, but occasionally to our frustration. Normal microbes help protect against attack by pathogens, and assist in the digestion of food, while we supply them with scraps to eat. Each of us harbors about 10^{15} bacterial cells. The number is ten times the number of human cells in our bodies; thus, in a sense we are more bacteria than human. Then again, our human cells are considerably larger, which means we may still refer to ourselves as Man or Woman: Measured as volume, our bodies are 99% *Homo sapiens.*

The important point is that all life on Earth is part of one giant web; thus, the biosphere can then be described as one single super-organism—by some referred to as Gaia.[15]

So we collaborate, but that does not mean we are unselfish; after all, a collaboration means there is something in it for us. Evolution demands any animal to have assertive and aggressive features—humans included. Consequently, our actions are often not beneficial to others; in fact, we are capable of bestial murders. The strange thing is that we may also sacrifice our lives for a stranger at the next corner. Evolution has apparently added more compassion to the human brain than to that of any other animal. The art of directing a society rests with the ability to stimulate the better aspects of our minds and to subdue the less constructive features.

Most nations work hard to fulfill this statement: Kindergartens, schools, churches, and mass media are prominent tools used to sway people in whatever direction is considered beneficial. And it works. It is certainly possible to make the population more friendly and empathetic, and to encourage compliance with both formal and in-

---

[15] For a recent update, see J. Lovelock, *The Revenge of Gaia* (2006).

formal rules of conduct. Some people refer to the mentality of the population as social capital. Obviously certain nations have been more successful than others in erecting this highly valuable sort of capital, and success depends both on the choice of values, or rules of conduct, and on how to implement them.

An understanding of human nature can serve as a starting point for this endeavor. In a way, we have an innate template for moral behavior, and this template offers a possible basis for establishing ethical rules. That is to say, our "moral sense" points toward what sort of directives are easier to implement. However, the point is definitely not just to follow what is natural, because quality of life is a

Symbolic figures of Christian morality.

better objective than biological success. Tenets that are less in tune with our innate tendencies can be accepted by the public, but for that to happen requires more effort.

The main point here is that input from science may help us decide what rules we ought to strive for. Religion, on the other hand, has an enormous potential when it comes to making people accept and obey rules of conduct.

––––––––

The concept of morality may depend on the question of whether we have a free will. If the genes control behavior, as is the case in lower animals, then any attempt at implementing particular rules of conduct would be meaningless. Consequently, a first issue is to consider to what extent our actions are programmed or predetermined in a way that restricts our chance to exercise honorable behavior. In short, do we really have free will?

The answer is that humans have more power to take control over their deeds than any other species. Our innate predispositions do have a word or two to say, but in most cases the individual is in a position to refrain from listening. Thus, the answer to the above question rests with how free the will should be in order to qualify as "free." In the end we are dealing with a semantic issue—and we do have a sufficient dose of free will to decide whether the more constructive answer is "yes" or "no."[16]

True, the process of evolution has made us a lot more independent of genetic directives compared with other animals, but at the same time there are obvious limitations. We simply cannot fly like a bird, or follow a scent like a dog. Furthermore, evolution has implemented a range of feelings and emotions that have a definite impact on our conduct. Normally we get angry when experiencing abuse, and we are inclined to help those we care about. It is possible to overrule our emotions, but it requires a resolute conscious effort and considerable determination. Consequently, the behavior of the average person, in the average culture, will tend to reflect the sort of propensities presented by the genes.

To conclude, within vague limits set by our genes, we are capable of choosing our actions, and within the scope of these limits we should be considered responsible for what we do. This freedom of

––––––––

[16] For a discussion on the neurological correlate of free will, see P. Haggard, "The Sources of Human Volition," *Science* 324 (2009): 731–33.

choice covers most ethical issues; thus, our dose of free will is definitely sufficient to warrant a discussion of morality.

Our freedom of choice is based on a feature I touched on in the last section: consciousness. When awareness is turned off, one does not possess any influence on one's body. A sleepwalker may perform acts that would never take place while awake; in fact, people have been acquitted of serious offences for that reason. Morality is only useful as a concept when the brain has turned on its capacity for consciousness. Yet, our mindful actions are always based on an interplay between the conscious and subconscious parts of the brain. Both are involved in evaluating sensual input and in consulting the enormous library of information laid down in the form of memory. Our conscious self is consequently just one of the players in decision making; it does have the power of influence, and usually it has the power of veto, but we typically take the leads suggested by a partly subconscious process without extensive deliberation.

———

Many people consider morality to be a uniquely human phenomenon, in stark contrast to all sorts of beasts, which live in a selfish world continuously fighting each other. The ancient Romans claimed that outside their cultivated world even humans lived according to the principle *homo homini lupus* ("man is like a wolf toward each other").[17] Their point was that in the absence of the formal rules of civilized society, people would not hesitate to kill fellow humans. Similar thoughts have characterized folklore for centuries: The notions of club-swinging Stone Agers, brute savages, and ever-fighting tribal people may be losing ground, but they have not vanished. Moreover, even people with liberal attitudes seem to assume that animals lack empathy and consideration. This is wrong. In many species, individual animals do indeed care about each other.

Whether morality really is a uniquely human quality is in the end a semantic question. Animals, particularly among the primates, show conduct reflecting what we consider ethical: They share food, support sick members of the flock, and hesitate to hit someone who is down. Chimpanzees have even been observed displaying what ap-

---

[17] The phrase seems a bit strange considering that the Roman Empire, according to legend, was founded by Romulus and Remus—twins who were saved and brought up by a self-sacrificing she-wolf.

pears to be moral indignation—"complaining" to other chimps that an ally has failed to fulfill his terms in connection with reciprocal altruism. Obviously, the behavior of chimpanzees is different from that of humans, or of gorillas, in the same way that our noses have distinct, species-specific characteristics. Both noses and propensities for behavior, including those reflecting moral tendencies, are shaped by evolution; and we are different branches on the tree of life. But if one chooses to use the term "nose" for what appears in the middle of the face of a chimpanzee, one may also choose to use "moral" when describing aspects of their behavior, because in both cases we are looking at traits with a shared evolutionary background.[18]

According to the Bible, God wrote His commandments and handed them to Moses some three- to four-thousand years ago. Some people consider the event to mark the introduction, or even invention, of moral rules. Actually, the basic principles of ethics were invented by evolution and date back millions of years, which is why we find related behavior in animals. In other words, a select set of species has evolved the propensity to care about the welfare of others. The Ten Commandments and similar scriptures are just a specification, and an expansion, of properties already laid down in our brains. The question of moral tendencies in animals is important because it helps us understand just what sort of properties we are equipped with, and thus what sort of mental resources are available for those who try to enhance compassionate behavior. (A further discussion can be found in *Do Animals Have Morality?*, below.)

Do Animals Have Morality?

Darwin once described a revelation he had when visiting the local zoo. He stopped by the cage of an orangutan called Jenny. One of the caretakers pretended to give the female ape an apple,

---

[18] F. de Waal is an expert on apes and in my mind the person who has written most intelligently on the biology of moral behavior. I recommend his *Primates and Philosophers: How Morality Evolved* (2006), and *The Age of Empathy: Nature's Lessons for a Kinder Society* (2009). For those who prefer a similar treatise written by a philosopher, I suggest R. Joyce, *The Evolution of Morality* (2006).

but subsequently refused to part with the fruit. Jenny behaved like a kid subjected to severe injustice; she threw herself to the ground, screaming and kicking. What Darwin suddenly realized was that the animal indeed had a typical human type of experience: It did feel wronged. The orangutan had a sense of justice. The obvious conclusion being that if these animals cared about fairness, then the associated feelings would necessarily reflect an innate tendency. In other words, morality reflects predispositions laid down in our brains by evolution.

It soon became clear to Darwin that many of the aspects considered as relevant for ethical judgment are based on innate tendencies. The capacity for compassion, for example, is common among mammals. It is observed most clearly in the relationship between mother and child, but adults too sometimes help each other. In fact, all the cornerstones of morality appear to be rudimentarily present in other species as well. In animals, however, these rudiments are presumably to a larger extent a question of instinctive tendencies rather than conscious decisions. Thus, one may choose to restrict the word "morality" to species with a certain level of self-awareness and free will. The point here is that both morality and free will are a question of more or less, rather than either/or. These features gradually appear when moving from monkeys to apes and then on to humans. Thus, the question of whether animals have morals appears to be a question of how conscious the choices need to be in order to refer to unselfish acts as based on ethical choices rather than on instincts. In my mind, apes would at least qualify.

Although we do have an innate template for distinguishing between good and bad, it is still a property that needs to be cultivated and encouraged. If the Romans had made an effort to retain moral values, then perhaps the Roman Empire would not have disappeared in a torrent of dissension and decay—whereas the so-called "primitive" tribal people endured.

———

The template for ethical behavior rests primarily with our emotional tendencies. It is the feelings evoked by various actions that spur our opinions as to what is right or wrong.

Two types of information help us understand what this template is about: One option is to learn to know the feelings that impact on moral choices. The other option is to compare moral rules in different societies: Features that appear independently in several places are likely to be based on innate predispositions rather than just cultural innovation. By exploiting this type of information, scientists have suggested that intuitive ethics rests on five pillars; that is, the template is based on feelings associated with the following issues:[19]

1. Care and compassion. The underlying feelings can be evoked by a range of ethical dilemmas, including those associated with sexual and environmental problems.
2. Justice and reciprocity.
3. Loyalty to the group.
4. Submission to hierarchies and respect for authority.
5. Purity, by which I mean avoiding disgust. A wide range of aversions may be included here.

Given that they are interpreted correctly, these five pillars should cover most ethical concerns. In the end, they are all based on properties laid down by the process of evolution. They do not offer any precise answers as to what is right or wrong, but act as an impetus behind the development of more detailed moral values. All of them allow for considerable variation as to rules of behavior, but at the same time they explain why we feel that moral features from a wide range of cultures are familiar.

———

It is well accepted that the brain has a template for language. Children attain the ability to talk and to understand what other people are saying without subjecting them to any formal training. What they need is to hear the spoken word, particularly during a critical period starting when they are a year or two old and lasting to the age of seven. Everyone possesses the capacity to understand how sounds can be meaningful by applying certain semantic and grammatical rules, but exactly what language a child learns depends of course on what the child hears.[20]

---

[19] J. Haidt and C. Joseph have written extensively on the foundation of morality, such as "Intuitive Ethics: How Innately Prepared Intuitions Generate Culturally Variable Virtues," *Daedalus* 133 (2004): 55–66; and J. Haidt, "The New Synthesis in Moral Psychology," *Science* 316 (2007): 998–1002.

[20] Learning to read and write is a different matter, as the written language is a cultural invention rather than a feature installed by evolution.

Many scientists assume that there is a parallel in how children learn ethics: We are born with a template for morality vaguely resembling that for language. Yet, the moral template is primarily associated with emotional and motivational propensities and is probably less tangible than the language template; that is to say, the underlying neurological modules are more dispersed and to a lesser extent dedicated to the exact purpose of creating moral behavior. Still, there are several similarities: A child learns what is right and wrong by observing the behavior of others and only partly by being told. Moreover, ethical rules become a sort of grammar, but instead of directing speech, they direct interactions with fellow human beings.[21]

Any adult can learn a new language or a new set of conventions to abide by. Infants, however, not only pick up things much faster, but the information obtained at that age is what really sticks. Childhood is consequently a very important period for the promotion of useful rules of conduct.

For an adult it is easy to participate in a conversation in one's mother tongue; subconscious parts of the brain take care of grammatical rules as well as the motor control of the various muscles involved in speech. We have similar modules in the brain that support our intuitive apprehension of moral issues. If we see someone throwing a stone at a defenseless child, we react emotionally without any need to contemplate further on the situation. Yet, in the same way that it is preferable to think before we talk, we do have the option to evaluate a challenging situation before we act.

What we learn as an adult is somewhat different. If we have just started to master Japanese, the conversation requires a great deal more mental effort. Likewise, if we have to adjust to novel rules of conduct, more care and conscious consideration are needed to avoid breaking the rules. Most people have experienced this observation when visiting a foreign country.

Our moral template is reasonably flexible; each culture erects its specific assortment of rules onto this template. Is there any reason to suggest that certain forms of guidance and directives are more constructive than others? I shall argue in favor of the answer being "yes."

---

[21] J. Mikail, "Universal Moral Grammar: Theory, Evidence and the Future," *Trends in Cognitive Sciences* 11 (2007): 143–52.

On the East coast of Honshu, Japan.

One concern that probably should be taken into consideration is that it is easier to install rules of conduct that comply more closely with our innate template. A house serves as an analog: It is possible to erect a building that stands partly outside the walls of its foundation, but the construction is more stable if placed right on top of the foundation.

Another point is that the rules should preferably adapt not only to the emotional basis constituting the template, but also with other aspects of the nature of being human. One may argue that the ethics should not deviate unnecessarily from our innate tendencies of behavior. The argument is related to the previous discussion of

stress caused by discord aspects of modern living. Enforcing rules
that go against basic instincts tends to cause frustration. On the
other hand, although one ought to take our innate nature into consideration, this does not imply that ethical rules should uncritically
reflect our behavioral propensities. The purpose should be to stimulate the positive qualities of human mentality, and subdue our more
dubious features: Violence ought to be suppressed and compassion
enhanced. The "eye-for-an-eye" type of justice may appeal to our
sense of fairness and be in tune with our innate moral template, but
it is not necessarily beneficial for society.

Ethics is to a large extent a question of the priorities of society.
In my mind the paramount objective of morality should be to improve the overall quality of life of the population, but that statement offers no more than vague guidance when it comes to formulating rules of conduct. Moreover, on certain issues the innate template for morality may stand counter to this objective.

One illustrative example involves a well-known ethical thought
experiment. You are watching a railway and suddenly spot a train
moving toward five people working on the rails. The only way to
avoid the train from killing the group is to push the switch so that
the train runs down a sidetrack where only one person will be
killed. Most people will here follow the rule of greater good and
press the switch. On the other hand, if the option is to push a person in front of the train in order to stop it from killing the five
workers, more people will opt from refraining. In the latter case as
well, the principle of optimal good would demand that you kill that
one person, but our innate template for moral behavior appears to
protest. The minor difference is that the latter action is deemed as
more violent or murderous, which causes people to refrain from
choosing this alternative.[22]

To some extent, rules of ethics ought to adapt to the innate
template, even though in certain cases one might have preferred to
push the rules toward a more rational stance. There are no clear-cut
answers as to what is optimal. Moreover, existing cultural attributes
have to be taken into account as well; abrupt changes are difficult to
implement and cause stress. Still, the long-term strategy may be to

---

[22] Philippa Foot first posed this ethical dilemma in an essay, "The Problem of Abortion and the Doctrine of the Double Effect" (1967), originally
called the "Trolley Problem."

move all cultures toward rational choices aimed at an optimal average quality of life.

In order to expand on the issues raised above, I shall examine a couple of examples in more detail.

Racial conflicts are illustrative. It is in human nature to make a clear distinction between "us" and "them." As a default, we are inclined to place strangers in a group called "them," particularly if they stand out as dissimilar (for example, due to skin color). They are consequently not included among those we care about.

Even if this tendency is understandable in light of our genetic inheritance, that does not mean we must comply and behave as racists. With a bit of conscious effort it is possible to alter this attitude; we can teach children that skin color is irrelevant. However, in a case like this we need to recognize that the rule we try to install runs partly counter to intuitive tendencies, and thus requires more in terms of a resolute intervention. In other words, when the rules of conduct we wish to introduce are less in tune with the template, it does not mean we have to give up, but we should be prepared to allocate more resources to the effort; for example, spending more time discussing the issue in schools.

The final moral pillar of those listed above—i.e., avoiding disgust—is highly relevant with regard to the relationship between or among groups of people. When anything is disgusting, it is because the brain assumes one should stay clear of it. If one finds food obviously putrid, one had better refrain from eating it because of the risk of disease. We also tend to consider any bodily fluids or excrement as repulsive, which makes sense because it may harbor pathogenic bacteria or viruses. The same is the case for animals that are likely to transmit diseases, such as rats or cockroaches. Thus, in most cases the feeling of disgust is rational; it reflects a universal feature of the human psyche, which primary function is to avoid pathogenic agents from reaching one's gut.

The expression "gut feelings" is derived from that. Originally it was a question of liking or disliking based on whether something is good or bad for us. We do, however, evoke gut feelings in cases that have nothing to do with the gut, or the risk of infections, and that are not necessarily rational. Many societies have, for example, the notion that menstruating women are unclean, and thus they should consequently be subject to particular rules, even though menstruation does not imply much of a risk for the transmission of pathogens. Moreover, the gut feeling originally designed to avoid dangerous food can also be employed when we want to distinguish between *them* and *us*. We can easily evoke aversion toward others simply by portraying them as disgusting, as when referring to people as vermin. Historically, this has been done, for example, in Nazi Germany and in the Hutu-Tutsi conflict in Rwanda. In both cases, the purpose was genocide by turning sentiment toward the idea that society ought to get rid of a certain population.[23]

—————

Sexual morality is another example worthy of closer examination. Most societies try to regulate sexual behavior, and in some cases the rules may be ready for a revision. In the Christian cultural tradition there has been a tendency toward considering almost any form of sexual activity as sinful. According to the Catholic Church, sex should only be allowed for the purpose of procreation; and then solely for properly married couples—covered by sheets and with the lights off.

Most mammals would feel at home in the Church. The problem is that of the two species that are not fit to be Catholics, one is *Homo sapiens.* The other is the bonobo of the genus *Pan* (that also includes the common chimpanzee). In these two species of primate, evolution has shaped sexual propensities to serve purposes beyond procreation: Sex is a means to establish close ties between individuals. In the case of the bonobos, it is question of creating a well-functioning band of animals—consequently everyone has sex with everyone, regardless of gender, and particularly in times of tension. In the case of humans, sex appears to serve the purpose of bringing male and female together in a more lasting bond.

A restrictive sexual morality is probably a consequence of two peculiar features: For one, the urge to engage in sex is arguably the most potent emotional instigator of behavior in the human mind; it has a strong and deep-seated foothold within the subconscious domain. The second feature is the drastic rise in the size of society, beginning with the invention of agriculture.

—————

[23] For a more extensive treatise on disgust, see D. Jones, "The Depths of Disgust," *Nature* 447 (2007): 768–71.

In tribal communities people tend to behave honorably, at least toward tribal mates, because reputation and good relations matter so much. If a man were to commit an atrocity toward a woman, everybody would know and the perpetrator would risk expulsion. People do not know each other in a city. The lack of close ties makes it easier to get away with offensive behavior. Moreover, large-scale societies imply an increased risk of spreading sexually transmitted diseases, and of causing pregnancy where the child would be left without a father. In other words, by moving away from tribal society, the sexual urge became more of a problem; the typical response was to introduce a stricter code of behavior, as reflected in the rules of most present-day societies.

Today, however, the problems associated with a more open and natural attitude to sex are partly cared for. By using contraceptives it is possible to avoid unwarranted pregnancies as well as preventing sexually transmitted diseases; moreover, we have a police force that can help reduce the danger of assault. This is not to say that sexual behavior is no longer the cause of problems, but we have means to reduce the negative consequences that were unavailable a couple of thousand years ago. Catholic morality dates back to this period, which is why it might be relevant with a revision in the direction of more acceptance for the nature of human sexuality.

One reason for modifying an overly suppressive sexual morality is that the suppression itself tends to cause stress and frustration. A greater acceptance for the underlying natural inclinations installed in humans would hopefully reduce the frustration, and possibly also reduce the risk of offensive behavior. Moreover, sexual pleasures are among the most potent brain rewards, and, when engaged in intelligently and empathetically, definitely among the more healthy choices of enjoyment.

———

It appears as though people take more pleasure in hugging than hitting each other. In fact, as pointed out by the Dalai Lama, people with compassion tend to be happy.[24]

The above observations are far from obvious. Compared with compassion, aggressive behavior can be even more important for one's genes, so why doesn't the brain offer stronger rewards when

———

[24] D. Lama and H. C. Cutler, *The Art of Happiness: A Handbook for Living* (1998).

we exert ourselves? The evolutionary perspective on human behavior suggests a possible explanation, and that explanation is relevant in a discussion of ethics.

How much people enjoy the acts of either hugging or hitting may reflect at which point in our evolutionary history the underlying behavioral predispositions were installed. During the early days of mammalian evolution, propensities were laid down in the form of instinctive tendencies. Animals react to external stimuli without undue deliberation or sentiment. The lineage leading toward humans, however, eventually evolved a massive intellect combined with a solid dose of free will. As a result, instinctive tendencies did not function that well; they were too easily overruled by the will. Evolution possibly responded to this problem by increasing the potency of brain rewards and punishment. If, for example, apples proved to be a useful element of nutrition, it became more productive to install positive feelings associated with the sight and taste of apples, rather than installing an apple instinct.

Aggression has a very long evolutionary history, consequently it is likely to be based primarily on instinctive tendencies rather than rewarding sensations. If someone steps on our toes, we probably react with immediate anger, not because we consider that to be an appropriate response, or because we enjoy our rage, but because someone hit the right button. Our sociable nature, on the other hand, came later—most likely after we split with the gorillas, as suggested by the observation that among our ape relatives, the chimpanzees and bonobos, are very social. It means that the major development of this feature occurred over the last five million years. At this point human evolution had turned to incentives rather than instincts, which would explain why most of us tend to prefer hugging and agree with the statement that the greatest pleasure is to please others.

Based on the above theory, it offers more in terms of satisfaction to help others rather than to fight them—even though, in many situations, our genes might be better off by the opposite type of action. In other words, by stimulating compassion and collaboration we not only improve society, but actually improve the life quality of the individual as well.

In fact, the main evolutionary purpose of our moral template is to organize interactions among people. The emotions associated with positive forms of interaction are coupled with potent brain rewards; consequently, social life in general is highly important for our quality of life. As suggested by the Roman politician Cicero, "If you share your life with a friend, you will have twice the joy and half the pain."

Positive human relations are the most important feature of an agreeable society. At the same time social life may be the Achilles heel of the modern world. Creating the kind of bonds we humans had in the Stone Age tribal setting is probably the most difficult and most important challenge we face. Industrialized society is not compatible with small groups of people having exclusive and lifelong relationships with each other. A suitable set of moral rules is a necessary premise for finding the optimal solution to this quandary.

Feelings such as guilt, shame, and a bad conscience are tools installed by evolution to encourage people to accept prevailing ethics. They are typically deemed to be disagreeable, and as such act as brain punishments in the present terminology. According to the principles of Darwinian Happiness, they are to be avoided. Luckily, decent behavior is all that is required to evade these feelings. On the other hand, for the sake of the common good, society should refrain from unwarranted stimulation of shame and guilt—after all, they are unpleasant. We need sensible rules, rules that people consider meaningful and that they obey without undue dilemmas. I believe most countries would be served by taking a rational approach and reconsider their ethics in light of present knowledge.

———

Religion has been a main player in the task of erecting and sustaining codes of ethics in most societies. The morality of Western countries is formed to a large extent by sentiment belonging to the Jewish-Christian cultural tradition. Presently, religion may be somewhat less important as an instrument to make people behave, since secular laws and concomitant enforcement are taking on some of the burden, but faith still has a lot to offer.

People are probably more likely to follow directives based on "God can see you" than based on "the police can see you." It does not require extensive intelligence to figure out that even the long arms of law enforcement are not always within an arm's length distance from you; but for those with a relevant belief, an omnipresent God can indeed "see" what you are up to. In fact, whether you are religiously inclined or not, the conscience evoked by the idea that "God knows" is in some cases sufficient to restrain people from doing anything wrong. The point was made in an experiment where people were given the chance to cheat on a task, when assuming no one would know. But after having been given a short talk that either included, or did not include, the sentence "God can see you." Even people who claimed not to be religious were influenced by the message in that they proved less likely to cheat.[25]

In tribal society, moral behavior was presumably governed to a large extent by the close ties among members. To have people really depend on each other and trust in each other is a sure way to improve conduct. We cannot reinstall the tribal way of life—at least not entirely. We will have to make the best of a society where the members are not that close. It means that we need formal laws. Yet, there is every reason to support informal rules of conduct and obedience based on individual evaluation of what seems right or wrong. Most people prefer to act according to their personal notions of correct behavior, rather than because certain alternatives carry a threat of punishment. Moreover, it may help if more people would consider the unwritten rules to be laid down by God—since pleasing God is pleasing for the adherent as well.

One concern about religious morality is that the rules have a tendency to be conservative. Society moves on while religions are stuck with commandments written ages ago, and therefore tend to be outdated.

Although the dominating creeds of today to some extent reflect this point of view, it is not obvious that religion has to be particularly conservative. It is possible to imagine a faith that is at least as adaptable as non-religious institutions. In fact, within the scope of Christianity there are congregations that stand out as highly progressive and radical in terms of present ways of thinking—for example, the Unitarian Universalists. On the other hand, it is not obvious that either the written, or unwritten, rules on which society depends should be too easily transformed. Continuity is important. If the rules change too fast, there will be a considerable discrepancy between the ethical rules of different generations. As previously pointed out, the codes you learn during infancy tend to stick, and a

---

[25] H. Phillips, "Is God Good?" *New Scientist* (September 1, 2007): 32–36.

discrepancy between consecutive generations may easily undermine the rules.

Listening to God's Whisper

I have tried to paint a picture of a Divine power that even the most scientifically minded atheist can accept; however, accepting that the term Divine can be applied to aspects of the Universe is not quite the same as perceiving and embracing God. Taking advantage of our religious propensity requires a bit more than mere acceptance. For those who are interested, science has some suggestions that may be helpful. I have previously argued that religious commitment can be useful both as to the quality of life of the individual, and in terms of benefits for society; the purpose of the last section of this chapter is to discuss what options are available for those who wish to tune into our internal voice of God.

———

A scientific portrait of God may be useful for some people. For others it has no value, either because they do not wish to entertain the notion of spirituality at all, or because they have their own visions of God. For the latter, the portrait may actually be detrimental in that it conflicts with their ideas of what God is about.

There is a parallel to music. In some situations you may want to write down the notes, or characterize the sounds in terms of frequency and amplitude of sound waves. The real value of music, however, rests on an individual's capacity to engage in it—to sense and feel the sounds. The theory and the paperwork are for those with particular interests. One does not need to have any idea as to what music is about in scientific terms in order to enjoy it; in fact, focusing on the physical aspects may draw attention away from taking delight in what one hears.

The capacity to take pleasure in music differs among individuals. The same can be said about religion, but in both cases it is possible to improve this capacity. We have been given a genetic predisposition to appreciate both music and an affiliation with the Divine. Not only do they offer pleasure, but they can give you strength and add content to your life. Thus, there are reasons to learn to engage in both.

As a scientist I often wonder why religion and music mean so much to us; neither is required to fill our lungs or find food for our stomachs. It is possible to suggest certain biological advantages, however, that might help explain why evolution added these attributes to the human brain, but overall they are strange and unexpected features. Their considerable impact on human emotions and behavior makes them even more astonishing.[26]

The feeling of a Divine presence can be a fantastic experience. At the same time it is an experience that science, to some extent, is able to define and characterize. People of different religious traditions describe their encounters in ways that other devotees recognize. The conditions are typically depicted as exhilaration, or high spirits, with a gratifying sensation permeating the body. It can be ecstatic, where one almost explodes with joy, or more a question of inner peace and relief from stress. Some people sense that they are part of a greater whole, where they are united with all living beings, while others stress the closeness to God. The point is that there are certain recurring themes. Moreover, much of the variation in ways of relating to God is present within the different creeds, suggesting that the variation reflects personality factors rather than belief systems. The shared features indicate that religious experiences are based on innate features of the human mind. In fact, today we are beginning to understand more about which parts of the brain are involved.[27]

In scientific terms, the typical religious experience apparently causes diminished activity in certain parts of the left cortex associated with self-awareness. At the same time, a corresponding part of the right cortex is stimulated. The dislocation of activity between these two related areas may be a central feature when people experi-

---

[26] I have previously proposed some evolutionary advantages, but they do not seem to be of sufficient importance to warrant the fondness we have for religion and music. See B. Grinde, "How Can Science Help Religion Towards Optimal Benefit for Society," *Zygon* 40 (2005): 277–88; and B. Grinde, "A Biological Perspective on Musical Appreciation," *Nordic Journal of Music Therapy* 9 (2000): 18–27.

[27] For more on the neurology of religion, see E. G. d'Aquili and A. B. Newberg, *The Mystical Mind: Probing the Biology of Religious Experience* (1999); or M. Beauregard and D. O'Leary, *The Spiritual Brain: A Neuroscientist's Case for the Existence of the Soul* (2007).

A small church on the island of Naxos, Greece.

ence closeness to God. It has been suggested that the sense of unity with the Universe rests with this pattern of activity—that is, a downplay of the "self" as a central component of consciousness, and thus an opening for a wider perspective.

There are techniques that help us gain access to the "religious state of mind"—meditation for example. Meditation can actually be useful even in the absence of any religious motivation in that it facilitates stress relief, and as such may help you find the default state of contentment. Whether the meditative experience is considered religious or not is partly a question of the power of the sensations evoked, but primarily a question of what terms one chooses to apply when describing the ensuing mental state. (Various meditative techniques may offer the easiest access to religious awareness—a topic discussed further in Appendix VI: *Meditation,* p. 207.)

It is certainly possible to meditate without considering it a religious activity; yet, adding the spiritual dimension seems to enhance the experience. It may spur the meditation to be more intense and rewarding. The Divine perspective offers something that a purely secular approach cannot give us, or at least is less likely to bring. In fact, an experiment in which participants were taught meditations, either by including a religious justification or a purely secular explanation, concluded that the religious approach gave a better experience.[28]

Maharishi Yogi claimed that if he could make a sufficient number of people meditate, peace and happiness would descend on Earth. He is not the only one with those kinds of ideas; the city of Auroville in India has a similar manifesto. The inhabitants try to induce what they refer to as "Divine consciousness" in their citizens, assuming that if that state of mind is reached to a required extent, then other problems will, if not evaporate, at least find their resolution more easily.[29]

In the Tibetan tradition, it is customary to meditate on compassion. Apparently this works as a sort of brain exercise where the module underlying compassion is expanded, improved if you wish, with concomitant effects on behavior.

Perhaps some people are overly optimistic as to the potential of meditation, but the techniques do have a way of impacting on the human psyche. I personally believe meditation can help bring forth positive aspects of human mentality. Even if peace does not enwrap the globe, it will at the very least characterize the individual engaged in meditation.

---

[28] A. B. Wachholtz and K. I. Pargament, "Is Spirituality a Critical Ingredient of Meditation?" *Journal of Behavioral Medicine* 28 (2005): 369–84.
[29] For more on Auroville, consult http://www.auroville.org/

Apparently it is easier to develop a religious disposition if one is in company with other devotees. Churches, temples, and monasteries are built for this purpose. Their design is typically based on the intention to stimulate religious awe: There are spires rising toward heaven, as well as icons and effigies that inspire people to sense Divinity. Thousands of years of experience are put into the design, and not in vain; the buildings certainly have the potential of evoking feelings in those who are ready.

When people gather for religious purposes, certain elements related to worship are commonly included. Prayer is one example. For some devotees prayer may be the most important form of contact with God, and many prefer to pray together with fellow worshipers. Elements that are pleasing to eyes and ears are often included in the veneration. Song and music are particularly powerful ingredients; in fact, it seems rare to have worship totally devoid of pleasing sounds. Apparently the joy of the aesthetic elements adds positive qualities to the experience of Divine presence, and thus helps people engage in God.

Some religious traditions include the use of psychoactive substances; for example, in the form of cannabis, the peyote cactus, or psilocybin mushrooms. These substances do have the potential of inducing a state of mind that can be construed as being in touch with Divinity; however, non-chemical approaches are not just safer, but in less danger of exposing the practitioner to the wrath of society.[30]

There are indeed several approaches toward experiencing Divinity. As pointed out by Christians, there are several paths to salvation. Those with a more atheist view of life may prefer another way of phrasing it: There are several techniques that can be useful when attempting to enter the particular state of mind associated with religious experiences. My point is that the above statements are just alternative ways of expressing the fact that religion has something to offer.

---

[30] See R. E. Shultes and A. Hofmann, *The Botany and Chemistry of Hallucinogens* (1991); or for a more recent treatise, R. R. Griffiths, W. A. Richards, U. McCann, and R. Jesse, "Psilocybin Can Occasion Mystical-type Experiences Having Substantial and Sustained Personal Meaning and Spiritual Significance," *Psychopharmacology* 187 (2006): 268–83.

Many people have a special feeling for nature; and some, including me, consider this to be a religious experience. When walking in the forest around my house, I sense a closeness and relatedness to other living organisms, and I consider that sensation to be directed toward God. It is definitely a feeling connected with joy. You can appreciate nature without adding any religious significance to it, but by seeing a Divine dimension the experience may prove even more exhilarating. Anyone can try to tune into this way of experiencing the environment; for those who do not have access to nature in the outdoors, caring for potted plants in the kitchen is an alternative. It is tempting to point out that the sense of humility and oneness with other life forms, which many people experience when outdoors, seems rational if accepting that life is part of a Divine creation. In a sense, venerating plants and animals is a way of worshiping the Creator. And although one does not need to evoke any Supreme Being in order to revere nature, the religious sentiment is likely to boost support for conservation efforts.[31]

We are all different. The intensity of people's experience of either nature or Divinity varies, as do the words one chooses to describe these feelings. The important point is that most people have something to gain by seeking the Divine aspects of life.

---

[31] Some people refer to the religious feelings evoked by nature as religious naturalism; alternatively, for those who prefer a less religious interpretation, as biophilia. See, for example: K. E. Peters, *Dancing with the Sacred: Evolution, Ecology and God* (2002); or B. Grinde and G. G. Patil, "Biophilia: Does Visual Contact with Nature Impact on Health and Well-being?" *International Journal of Environmental Research and Public Health* 6 (2009) 2332–43.

CHAPTER FIVE

The closed and the open gateway. From the ancient city of Termessos, Turkey.

Heaven On Earth

Where Do We Stand?

I have argued that in order to improve conditions on this planet, it is important that we gain as much knowledge as possible concerning both the Universe and its human component. Moreover, if we are able to direct attention to whatever stands behind our Universe, we gain access to a feature of the human mind with considerable potential. For me, the above statement stands as our best chance at creating heaven here on Earth.

Many people refute the existence of God. I would hope that Divinity, as described in this book, will find acceptance with most people, although approval may require the openness of a true scientific mind. It is perhaps more difficult for an atheist to engage in more elaborate belief systems, but, as I shall argue, it may be worth a try.

The first brains created by evolution were very simple. They registered certain features of the environment and passed on relevant instruction to the muscles without any forms of contemplation. The human intellect popped up as a byproduct of an evolutionary adaptation toward improving the response of the individual to environmental cues. Evolution never focused on creating a brain proficient in mathematics or science, but solely on a brain more capable of promoting the underlying genes. Consequently, although we have considerable analytical capacity, the outcomes of our analyses are not always logical or optimal. The emotional components of the brain have not vanished; but they do have a considerable impact on behavior as well as on ways of thinking.

People generally agree with the statement that most people do not behave rationally, while having more of a problem with the notion that their own behavior is not always that rational either. Then again, logical rationality is not necessarily always the best choice.

A systematic, scientific approach is useful in many situations. If the task at hand is to build a bridge, then a technical stance is required. The point is that our capacity to solve problems in a scientific way is just one of several features included in the brain. Emotions reflect a more fundamental feature of the mind; and they are what brought us genetically to where we are today. Science and engineering are byproducts that appeared after evolution had given us our present set of genes. I maintain that, when evaluating rationality as opposed to emotions, the foremost issue is: Which option best serves our quality of life? At least in certain situations, emotions trump rationality. Are you, for example, scientifically minded when you fall in love? And should you be? Is it your logical capacity that allows you to enjoy art and music? And does it matter? Of course you can approach these issues in a scientific manner, but I believe that approach may simply limit the joy you are able to harvest.

Robert Pirsig claimed that "When one person suffers from a delusion, it is called insanity. When many people suffer from a delusion it is called a Religion."[1]

My sentiment is that faith in God can do you good, and as such can be a highly rational choice, although some of the doctrines promoted by certain creeds are less useful. The main point here is that irrationality occasionally serves you well. We all have our peculiar conceptions and fantasies. The ones associated with belief in God are not necessarily more absurd than those concerning other aspects of life.

If you are lucky, you might very well consider your spouse to be the best person in the world. Fortunately, that is difficult to disprove; yet, objectively speaking, the number of competitors would make it highly unlikely. Thus you may be wrong, but you are advised not to change your conceptions, because the notion that your wife or husband is number one is likely to serve you best.

Quality of life does not depend on objectivity; in fact, succumbing to irrational, emotional sentiments can often improve our lives. Sometimes it is better to daydream, or engage our capacity to rationalize or suppress disagreeable facts. We ought to retain a belief in ourselves even if everything turns against us. The principle applies to the way we relate to God as well; our portrait of God serves us best if colored by feelings rather than rationality. In short, *in my mind it is irrational to strive toward being completely rational.*

---

[1] Pirsig is primarily known for the book *Zen and the Art of Motorcycle Maintenance* (1974).

The sciences sometimes have a problem seeing the forest and not just the trees. They are good at describing the details, but may miss the deeper potential of the whole. Religions may miss the trees but point to the forest because they do not fit religious visions; nevertheless these visions help people sense an overarching entity. I believe the art of living rests with *seeing* the trees, yet *sensing* the forest.

Another feature of the sciences is that they are not necessarily tuned toward helping people, but focus instead on explaining reality as objectively as possible. This is not criticism; it is the way it ought to be. We need basic research that is not aimed at any particular objective. For the typical scientist, knowledge has intrinsic value; for me, the process of increasing my understanding of nature is associated with great joy.

Scientists, however, might try to keep in mind that for most people other aspects of existence are more important. And in the end, science *should be* evaluated with respect to how it contributes to human life. Explaining the cosmos or the inner workings of a cell are the means, but the real value of insight rests with the capacity to improve quality of life. This contribution has proven to be monumental—unfortunately for both good and bad. We have learned to cure or alleviate a long list of diseases, but we have also constructed a wide assortment of deadly weapons of war and deeply wounded our environment.

I mentioned in the Preface that God might be subjected to "A Day of Judgment for the Divine," and that I believe God would pass the trial. What about the sciences? Will they stand proud on their Day of Judgment? Are people really happier today than in the Stone Age thanks to the knowledge science has produced? The answer is not obvious, because the voices of those who died in wars and holocausts made possible by human ingenuity are not heard, while those who were cured by modern medicine will be heard. Personally, I believe science has done much more good than bad, but then again I am a scientist.

Both science and religion have great potential for improving our lives, and both are easily misused. The important issue, therefore, is how to make the most of them. Thus, whether it is God or Science we put up for judgment, we should be concerned not so much with the past but with their potential for serving mankind in the future.

Perhaps we can learn from our mistakes; perhaps we shall be able to exploit the advantages and avoid some of the pitfalls. It all depends on how intelligent the human race actually proves to be.

———

Like everyone else, scientists have a tendency to follow fashions. The present trend is to consider the notion of a Divine force as unscientific—the word "God" has become heretical.

Fashions change. In 1783 John Michell, a British natural philosopher, suggested that there are stars with so high density that light cannot escape due to the force of gravity.[2] He referred to them as "black stars." He was not taken seriously. For about two hundred years his name was forgotten, but he was right. In the 18th century, people could safely scorn his ideas, for not only did the notion of black holes sound crazy, but it was impossible to test whether they existed or not. If light cannot escape, then the object would necessarily not be visible. Black holes are indeed not visible, but science has found indirect ways of proving their existence. We know where they are because they bend the light of more distant stars, and because they impact on the trajectory of surrounding objects.

Those who read what Michell wrote in 1783 may claim that he was wrong, because black holes are not stars. This is a semantic issue, just as, in a way, is the question of God's existence. Black holes are not stars, if one defines stars as objects emitting light; they are sort of "dead" stars. Today we know a lot more about the nature of black holes, so part of what he wrote is outdated; yet in principle he was right.

Do we have here a parallel to the idea of a Divine Force?

Obviously we cannot see God, but perhaps we can infer the existence of something Divine in other ways. God may prove to be a constructive concept; not just because a belief in God may help society, but because the concept actually is relevant for our interpretation of reality as it offers a kind of explanation for the existence of the Universe: The Force referred to as God made it happen. Some people probably feel that this may improve the model we have of the Universe.

———

[2] For a description of Michell's theory, see M. Kaku, "Will We Ever Have a Theory of Everything," *New Scientist* (November 18, 2006): 62–65.

In future, the description of Divinity will probably differ from the portrait delivered on these pages, but I believe the principles outlined will remain. Black holes and God share the attribute that we will never see them, never touch them, but they still have a correlate in reality; that is, they can be experienced indirectly: black holes due to their impact on the surroundings, and God by our sensing of the Creation.

The famous philosopher Auguste Comte (1787–1857) claimed in 1825 that we will never know what the sun consists of because it is impossible to go there and find out. He was right in his conjecture that we cannot go there and pick up a sample; any Earth-made objects would simply melt and burn. While it took two hundred years for Michell's theory to be justified, Comte's claim was proven wrong just two years later when scientists realized we can give an accurate description of what the sun is made of simply by analyzing the atomic signature in the light emitted. Today we know what is inside the sun.

Michelangelo painted his "God" with an outstretched hand reaching toward "Man." Figuratively speaking, that may happen but physically one might as well try to touch the sun. It is impossible. For many people, however, the "light" they sense as emitted by God is all the contact they need.

———

Richard Dawkins has been referred to as the chief gladiator of science in the battle with religion. I appreciate that he has also made the following statement:

> I accept that there may be things far grander and more incomprehensible than we can possibly imagine.... My mind is open to the most wonderful range of future possibilities, which I cannot even dream about, nor can you, nor can anybody else. What I am skeptical about is the idea that whatever wonderful revelation does come in the science of the future, it will turn out to be one of the particular historical religions that people happen to have dreamed up. ... If there is a God, it's going to be a whole lot bigger and a whole lot more incomprehen-

sible than anything that any theologian of any religion has ever proposed.[3]

In other words, Dawkins opens the door to the possibility for the existence of an entity that may be referred to as God. I agree. And if Dawkins is open to this option, it appears to me that most people might be able to embrace the possibility of something Divine.

Of course, the images and texts describing God carry the stamp of human creativity. They were formed by humans. Our imagination is adding life to something that would otherwise seem void and lifeless. But in the same way that there is a canvas beneath the oil used to paint a picture, there is something Divine underneath our sensations and conceptions of God. Although the canvas on which we portray the Divine seems empty and boring without any paint, it does not necessarily mean that God has no qualities that may be of interest, but simply that we are unable to have more than a vague perception of what Divinity is really all about.

According to the Bible, the Kingdom of God is inside you.[4] The sensation of Divinity is a potential that exists within each and every one of us. We can seize the opportunity, enter the spiritual realm, and thus transform ourselves. Or we can shut it out. We humans can certainly survive without experiencing God, just as we can survive without love. People have even tried to establish nations without any allusion to religion—although without much success. For example, in 1967 Enver Hoxha proclaimed that Albania was the first atheist nation. "If anything is to be worshipped, let it be me," he supposedly declared. Hoxha soon became unpopular. After his death in 1985, God swiftly returned to the scene; today, 70% of the population is Muslim and 30% Christian.[5]

---

[3] The quotes are from a discussion between Dawkins and Francis Collins set up by *Time* magazine and printed as their cover story for the November 5 issue of 2006.

[4] The relevant passage is in Luke 17:21. The text, however, is alternatively translated as "God's Kingdom is among you."

[5] More or less all the inhabitants are considered members of a religion, but, although most people may believe in God, few are fundamentalistic about it. Consequently, there is not much conflict between Muslims and Christians. Presumably people had similar religious convictions under Hoxha's rule that they would not dare to admit.

Religion is unlikely to disappear. The intelligent choice is to make the most of it. Philosophers in ancient India got the point. According to them there are two aspects of life that are important: One is to win the respect of fellow citizens; the other is to sense the unity with the Divine aspects of existence.

Where Do We Go?

I have suggested that science may help religion—by updating the story of Creation, by offering a backdrop for ethics, and by helping us sense the Divine. There is yet another domain in which many creeds are engaged, and where science may contribute. It is natural to want to know what is ahead. The Christian church, for one, has a tradition of presenting prophecies. Like many other spiritual movements, it tries to inform people as to what is going to happen. Science has something to say about the future, particularly in connection with the following three issues:

I. What happens when we die?
II. Where does the evolution of the human species lead?
III. What destiny befalls our planet and the Universe in the long run?

There is a fourth question that means a lot more—an issue reflecting the grandest and most difficult challenge mankind has ever faced:
IV. How will the global society of humans manage over the next hundred years?

If we prove able to offer all the inhabitants decent living conditions, we have in reality created Heaven on Earth; and people of today will lay the foundation for responding to this challenge. I shall discuss the first three issues before I consider the fourth question.

I. So, what happens when we die?
There is disagreement about whether or not there is some sort of spirit or soul that subsists after the body disintegrates. As a scientist, my immediate reaction is skepticism as to the existence of a soul that moves on to an afterlife, but then being a scientist may imply a bias against any such ideas. Moreover, spirit and soul are rather vague terms, and it is tempting to point out that parts of what

constitutes *us* as human beings, actually does move on. It may look as if the body disappears, with the bones lasting longer than softer tissue, but things actually do not disappear into nothing. Our bodies do not simply vanish; the atoms, and to some extent the molecules, still exist. In fact, the water molecules remain to a large extent intact, while the organic molecules are mostly broken down for the components to be re-utilized by other organisms. To the extent that "we," or our spirit, is associated with the atoms and molecules of our bodies, we may look forward to more or less eternal life. We just need to change shape occasionally—or reincarnate if you prefer that term. Indeed, the idea of reincarnation into other life forms makes sense in biological terms. Of course, we should not begrudge the idea of spending some intermittent time as bacteria, but then being a bacterium is nothing to be ashamed of.

Water offers an interesting illustration. Water molecules are occasionally broken down and reformed, but the majority presumably remains intact for thousands of years. Your body contains $2x10^{27}$ of them, and some are likely to have been present in the body of Jesus (or any other person living at that time). This statement is backed by a statistical analysis assuming the water molecules that passed through Jesus have since been dispersed evenly around the globe, which is a likely supposition.

It is not only our atoms that move on to future generations, but our children inherit our genes. Even in the absence of any children of our own, the genes may still move on as a considerable fraction of our genes (normally 25%) are present in the children of our siblings. We also leave other remnants that outdate our bodies: Family and friends are left with memories, and whatever we have constructed or achieved during our lifetime can remain or have an impact long after we are dead.

What about our souls going to Heaven?

Visions of an afterlife have probably been around for a long time. As mentioned previously, even the Neandertals buried their dead and apparently added flowers and artifacts. This observation suggests that they considered death to be a transition, and that they expected to get a second chance around—possibly a life in the Neandertal version of Heaven. As they split off from our ancestors half a million years ago, such religious notions probably date back even farther in time.

Holding the rock referred to as Krishna's Butterball,
near Mamallapuram, India.

In my mind, given the option of visioning a Heaven with an eternal life of joy, there is no obvious reason to abandon this prediction; after all, if nothing else, it may add something positive to our present life. In fact, a paradise in our minds can be worth even more than a paradise in afterlife, especially if our actual living conditions lack those qualities. Yet, whatever our destiny may be, there is every reason to try to make the most out of what is here and now.

II. Are humans an end product of the evolutionary process?

Definitely not! Evolution does not stop. Evolution is simply a question of who are begetting more children. If an individual, or a subpopulation, produces a lot of progeny, then their genes will constitute a larger fraction of the gene pool of the coming generation. The human species is defined by the total pool of genes contained in the population; any change in its composition implies an evolutionary modification. Consequently, if people with genes disposing for asthma or aggression beget more offspring, then these conditions are likely to be more common in the following generation. It is worth taking a closer look at this quandary.

Evolution is based on two principles: One, there are variations in genes due to mutations; and two, there is selection toward individuals with the "best" genes—that is, toward genes with the best capacity to procreate. Mutations can be considered random: Most of them have little if any effect, and a certain fraction is detrimental, but only rarely do mutations offer an advantage. If one stops selecting *against* genes disposing of various diseases, then the burden of disease will increase, simply because mutations are more likely to be detrimental than beneficial. As a consequence of modern health care, there are a number of conditions that are no longer selected against, such as asthma and nearsightedness. Fortunately human evolution is a slow process; thus, there may not be any drastic changes in our gene pool over the next thousand years. By the time negative changes have become troublesome, I hope we shall have found other means of dealing with the problem.

It is theoretically possible to take control over the evolutionary process. The technically and relatively easy solution is to establish breeding programs. We have proven the power of breeding in the case of farm animals, and humans are in principle no different. Modern biotechnology opens up the way for more advanced options: In the long run it may be technologically possible to do a genetic design of babies, which means adding or removing genetic dispositions according to defined preferences. However, it seems unlikely that this strategy will have any appreciable impact on the total pool of human genes. Moreover, any forms of tinkering with the genes are, at least for the time being, politically and ethically impossible. I am not sure I would wish to argue against that viewpoint.

Not only can the genes affecting health change, but so can genes affecting behavior and emotions such as compassion and hostility. Will the future population become more violent? The answer is that we do not know. The important point, however, is that the issue we ought to focus on does not relate to genetic changes. The challenges facing mankind rest with how we handle innate human behavioral tendencies as they are presently manifest in the world.

A pendulum can be used as an analogy in order to illustrate how our innate tendencies affect observed deeds. In the absence of any attempts to influence people's actions, behavior will reflect innate human nature, i.e., the "point of gravity," where the pendulum points straight down. Take, for example, our propensities to exhibit conduct that is either compassionate or unfriendly: The balance between the two will reflect the balance laid down by evolution—sometimes people are kind, sometimes hostile. It is, however, possible to move the pendulum, but that requires a resolute effort. We can pull the behavior toward the side of compassion, but the task goes against "gravity," so it is demanding. Our chance of success is best if we can get a good grip on the pendulum. In order to do so we need to know what we are up against—that is, we ought to understand how innate tendencies impact on our propensity to be sociable. Moreover, retaining the pendulum in the desired position requires continuous effort. The moment we release our grip, it is likely to swing back toward more hostility.[6]

One obvious way to move the pendulum toward compassion is to see that people are well adjusted and happy. Satisfied individuals tend to have more surplus energy to be used for the benefit of others. But improving the quality of life is not sufficient; it is also necessary to persuade them that, for their personal good, and for the good of society, they ought to be gregarious. Religion is a relevant tool in this context, but so are schools and mass media.

You may have heard the saying "history repeats itself." Human innate tendencies were involved in determining events a thousand years ago, and they will continue to have a say for the next thousand years. The pendulum may move, but it has a tendency to swing back and forth across the point of gravity. History repeats itself because events reflect human nature as it is played out. The cultural environment changes, but although the culture certainly has an effect on behavior, it does not change our innate predispositions. Which is why knowledge about human nature can help us not only to understand the past but also to forecast the future.

---

[6] For a more comprehensive discussion of the pendulum analogue, see B. Grinde, "Darwinian Happiness: Can the evolutionary perspective on well-being help us improve society?" *World Futures—The Journal of General Evolution* 60 (2004): 317–29.

The same knowledge, however, is also important if you want to change the course of history. The fact that evolution moves very slowly allows for a certain predictability about human behavior and a consistency in what factors will typically have an impact. Human behavior is not locked in a fixed position, but is malleable within vague confines. If we learn how to encourage compassion, then certain undesirable historical events may be less likely to be repeated.

III. What will happen to our planet and the Universe?

Five billion years from now the sun will increase in size to become a red giant. The problem is that the size will probably be sufficient to encompass the present trajectory of the Earth. The good news is that by then the sun will have decreased in mass, thus its gravitational force will have weakened and Earth will have consequently moved farther away, which means it may barely avoid being consumed by the sun. The sun will subsequently shrink in size, but once more it will grow and eventually reach the new orbit of Earth, pulling our planet into its burning inferno. When the temperature has reached half a million degrees Celsius, everything will evaporate, and Earth will become simply part of the superheated particle plasma of the sun. A dying sun that is.

Even if we should evade this prospect, life does not stand much chance. Soon after, the sun will have burnt most of its fuel and will have shrunk to become a white dwarf. Subsequently it will cool down gradually, and in the end will be as cold as the Universe itself. Thus, whether we first evaporate or not, the final destination is an ice-cold relic with a temperature similar to the average of the Universe: -270 °C.

Not that it matters much. We, or for that matter other life forms, are unlikely to hang around to witness these events. Today we worry that rising levels of CO_2 will increase the temperature to the effect of causing havoc to the climate and making things unpleasant for us humans. Looking further ahead, the bigger danger may be a depletion of CO_2. The higher temperature will cause increased weathering of rocks, and the concomitant release of silica should bind up CO_2—possibly more or less all of it. The problem then is that plant life depends on this component of the atmosphere, and if the plants disappear, so will O_2, which means that animals like us can no longer breathe. Some scientists suggest that within, say, 500 million years, all higher life forms will be gone. What may remain is the sort of life that started out on this Earth, bacterial-like cells living the same way as they did then at hydrothermal vents. Then, perhaps, the cycle of evolution will repeat itself. There should be time for one more such cycle before the sun devours the Earth.[7]

Another expected event that is likely to shake things up is a forthcoming collision between the Milky Way Galaxy and its closest neighbor, the Andromeda Galaxy. It is hard to foresee what the consequences will be, but one probably ought to look up for incoming stars and other cosmic objects.

Not even universes are expected to last forever. Previously it was estimated that the lifetime for our Universe was 20 billion to 30 billion years. The idea then was that everything moved apart for a good many years—i.e., cosmic expansion—before starting to contract. In the end, the Universe would return to the state of a single singularity, perhaps to give rise to a new universe. We humans, at least the scientists, like the idea of cycling events, because in that way we brush off the question of what was before the beginning or what follows after the end. This scenario, however, seems less likely today since it was recently discovered that the galaxies are actually moving apart at an *increasing* speed. According to present calculations, by the time the rate of expansion approaches the speed of light, everything will dissolve into elementary particles and radiation. The Universe will be smeared out over an enormous area. Apparently this is the diametrical opposite of a singularity; yet perhaps it is something similar.[8]

Given that expansion does not stop, astronomers see two alternative scenarios. One, the acceleration phase ends, but expansion does not stop, which means that in some 100 billion years the last star will burn out and we will be left with a cold and dark eternity. Before that time, however, the expansion may have gone so far that no planet (or star) has any chance of seeing or sensing its neighbors. Two, acceleration intensifies, and within 50 billion years dark energy tears everything apart—a "big rip" involving all structures from super-clusters of galaxies to atoms, which means that the Universe

---

[7] For more on this theory, read P. Ward, "Gaia's Evil Twin," *New Scientist* (June 20, 2009): 28–31.

[8] S. Battersby, "The Unraveling," *New Scientist* (February 5, 2005): 31–37.

returns to a soup of elementary particles, but this time an extremely diluted soup. The main alternative to these expansion scenarios is the aforementioned idea of a "big crunch": Everything goes back to a singularity, perhaps followed by a new Big Bang in an eternal cycle.

It is probably a bit premature to worry about the destiny of the Universe, or for that matter our planet. There is sufficient time left to enjoy life—not just for us, but for our descendants as well—if we can only tackle the more immediate perils.

———

The Universe began as a formless soup of energy and elementary particles, but developed into a highly elaborate cosmos. It is an incredible drama, whether or not you sense a Divine Force as the director. We humans have just arrived on the scene to play out our part. We have been put in charge of Planet Earth, and the question is: How will we carry out this role? The biggest issue facing this planet is what will human endeavor lead to over the next ten or hundred years. The future of mankind depends on the answer. Unfortunately, the future of individual humans does not depend on the answer.

Bacteria today presumably resemble the first forms of life that appeared three billion to four billion years ago; all other types of organisms are more recent settlers. Our human sense of justice advocates that whoever first settled on a piece of land has the right of ownership. Thus, if anyone ought to have proprietary rights, it is the bacteria. In fact, if there is one life form that is likely to subsist whatever the present management of Earth should infringe on the planet, it is the bacterial cells. The smallest are actually the strongest.

It has happened before. Some 250 million years ago the bacteria managed to strike back: About 90% of the animals became extinct. A range of volcanic eruptions probably triggered the event, but it is likely that the bacteria did their part by feeding on the sulfur released as a consequence of the eruptions thus producing massive amounts of hydrogen sulfide, which is toxic to animals. Something similar may happen again.[9]

———

[9] P. Ward, "Precambrian Strikes Back," *New Scientist* (February 9, 2008): 40–43.

Multicellular organisms dominate the life we can see. They comprise the more complex, more dramatic, and more intelligent forms of life. Bacteria, however, dominate in number (not counting viruses). They even dominate within your body: You move around with about ten times as many bacterial cells as human cells, suggesting that you might consider yourself primarily a bacterial life form. We pretend to own this planet, but the future will tell whether our intelligence is worth bragging about when compared to bacterial persistence.

IV. How will our global society of humans manage in the next hundred years? Were we given a paradise in order to first abandon it and then to destroy it?

For the last 100,000 years mankind has enjoyed excellent living conditions—at least biologically speaking. The population has gradually increased to an extent that has allowed us to colonize more or less all the dry land and eventually dominate the biological environment on all continents. I believe the Stone Age is grossly underrated, at least considering tribes possessing sufficient territory to carve out a decent living. Life expectancy was shorter, but primarily because various infections caused early death in those days, whereas today we have a cure for most ailments. Those who avoided disease presumably lived on to old age, as old as one can expect in the absence of hospitals and nursing homes. And they were probably at least as happy as we are.

Until 10,000 years ago people still lived the life evolution had shaped them for. They were hunter-gatherers, roaming around in tribes of perhaps 20 to 50 members. At that point, however, some of our ancestors left this "Garden of Eden" to create their own gardens. Farming marked the first step away from the environment of evolutionary adaptation.

Agriculture opened for large-scale societies with divisions of labor, and eventually for the exploits of science and industry. Subsequent progress has undoubtedly given us a lot in terms of consumer goods, but at a price. For instance, the population boom threatens to destroy the planet, and the discords associated with the present way of living cause physical and mental health problems. We have a system of health care with the potential to bandage most burdens, but it is only there for a fraction of the Earth's population, and wounds to the mind are difficult to cure. It is my hope that eventually we shall find ourselves in a new and even better Garden of Eden—a society built on the advantages of industrialized society, but with conditions of living that cater to the nature of being human. A society that offers everyone a chance to live a good life.

So far we have not made it. The present world is not a paradise—certainly not if you visit the severe drought areas of Africa or squatter towns around the globe. But there is no reason to give up; human ingenuity may just prove to be sufficient. In my mind there are three main pillars this ingenuity has to focus on: One, science as a means to understanding our planet and teaching us how to erect sustainable living conditions; two, learning how to deal with human nature, which in the end may prove to be the most difficult part; and three, opening up for Divinity as a helping force.

We are experts on technology—and technology is important. The future demands a vast array of advanced engineering. Yet, building bridges and sending people off to the moon or Mars are the easy tasks. This is not where the shoe pinches. Is it within the scope of science to find solutions to environmental issues and at the same time point out how we can produce sufficient amounts of food and gadgets to please the population? If we manage to restrict or restrain the numbers of people populating the Earth to a reasonable level, this should be possible. Actually, the present food production is more or less sufficient to go around, but the environment is already suffering under the strain of providing that much food. Engineers may find solutions that take care of the environment; but, as pointed out by numerous aid workers, distributing the food equitably is already encountering serious obstructions. To my mind the real problem goes a bit deeper. It is a question of how to deal with human nature: how to bring forth compassion and restrain violence; how to make people cooperate for a common good, while allowing everyone to seek their personal happiness; and, not least, how to restrict the size of the population.

Knowledge and insight are just tools. They are required to solve the challenges of engineering and the challenges of handling mankind. To reach the minds of billion of humans and have an impact on their behavior requires something more. Perhaps there is only one factor that carries that little extra momentum—God.

In Christian burials it is customary for the priest to declare "from dust to dust." We were born out of the Earth's soil and shall return to the soil. On a larger time scale, the priest may have stated "from stardust to stardust." The chemical elements within us were formed by the interior of a star, spread like dust upon the explosion of that star, and shall most likely again return to the burning interior of the sun.

In the meantime it is up to us to care for life on this planet. We have the power to create Heaven on Earth. We have the required intellect to solve problems and plan for the future—but human society may not move in the desired direction. We are standing on the edge of a knife, delicately balancing between heaven and hell. God may prove to be the extra weight required for the balance to tip in the right direction. Our capacity to sense a Divine Creator offers a helping hand, but the other hand needs to grasp the sciences. We need true knowledge to find the right path, and if we hold on to God there is a better chance we will actually be able to move down that path.

The monastery of Montserrat in Spain.

APPENDICES

A floating stage or an incomplete cross?

Appendix I:
Related Portraits

Christianity has extensive texts rich in doctrines and accounts written to enlighten the parishioners, as do other world religions such as **Islam**. These particular texts, however, are not needed in order to engage in a Divine Force; and I believe that not just atheists but also a fair number of believers are skeptical about their content. In fact, the majority of those who acknowledge an existence of God probably do not insist on the correctness of any ancient manuscript.

There are alternatives for those who prefer a less dogmatic faith. Some of these alternatives are considered independent religions, but they are typically not very visible. By not putting much energy into missionary work, they tend to fall behind in the global religious market; they drown in the noise made by the major belief systems. I shall briefly describe some of the relevant movements as they reflect views of the Divine related to my presentation.

Pantheism and **Panentheism** imply belief in God as a property of the Universe—a permeating spiritual Force that stands behind our existence. For pantheists, nature is God. The panentheists do not necessarily disagree, but they consider God as something slightly more than just a component of cosmos; they assume God exists outside, or above, the physical Universe. These types of faith are often associated with tribal people. Tribal religion may include a variety of legends, but the details of the anecdotes are rarely considered important. God's existence does not rest on the odd stories. For those who are less tribal, there is a world-wide pantheist congregation—at least in cyberspace.[1]

Deism began as an alternative to traditional Christianity in the 17th and 18th centuries.[2] It is a typical product of the Age of Enlightenment, when the Deists considered God to be the creator of the Universe, but assumed that God does not have any capacity to make an impact on the contemporary world. They see the Bible as a

---

[1] See http://www.pantheism.net/.
[2] T. Paine, *Age of Reason: Being an Investigation of True and Fabulous Theology* (in two parts: 1794, 1796).

text written by human beings, and thus not a direct reflection of the Divine. **Theism**, in its more basic form, sees a (single) interfering God, but does not require adherence to particular scriptures. In a way deism and pantheism are related, and similarly theism and panentheism.

Creationism and the related **Intelligent Design** (ID) are probably the movements that have received the most attention in recent years.[3] They are somehow a modern Christian response to the scientific attacks on biblical descriptions. Supporters point out how the Universe has been fine-tuned for the existence of life; they underline all the strange things that have happened on the evolutionary road to human beings and conclude that there are too many coincidences and unexplainable observations for a purely scientific account to have credibility. Thus, an intelligent, creative Force must be present for the model of reality to be complete.

The main problem with these movements, as I see it, is that at least some of the adherents try to defend the content of the Bible as being scientifically true. That, unfortunately, implies a disregard for an understanding of evolution. As an example, some advocates claim that evolution could not generate eyes, because it is difficult to envision the various intermediate stages required. However, eyes do not require a Divine miracle; their evolution can be explained reasonably well within the framework of evolutionary theory. Their disregard for science seems somewhat pointless. In fact, an offshoot of creationism known as theistic evolution fully accepts the paradigm of evolution and considers God to be an intelligent creator operating by means of the laws of nature.[4]

Agnosticism should also be mentioned in this overview.[5] The agnostics claim that it is impossible for us to tell whether there is a God or not. The attitude is definitely sensible, but personally I consider the indications available and sufficient to postulate the existence of something that may be referred to—and worshiped—as Divine. My stance, however, is partly semantic, partly personal.

---

[3] The following books present the ID movement: P. E. Johnson, *Darwin on Trial* (1991); and M. J. Behe, *Darwin's Black Box* (1996).
[4] See, for example, K. R. Miller, *Finding Darwin's God* (2000).
[5] The concept of agnosticism was introduced by the British biologist Thomas Huxley in 1869.

The trends mentioned above reflect common points of view rather than doctrines from major systems of faith. There are, however, established religions that accept these less dogmatic attitudes as to what God is about. For those like me, who sympathize with the notion of a God but require Divinity to be compatible with science, there are indeed creeds with reasonably open arms. Perhaps the more famous ones are the Unitarian church, Bahà'í, and **Buddhism**. Thus, the diversity of present religious movements seems to be sufficient for most people to find appropriate fellowship.

Prayer flags on top of a mountain in Bhutan.

The author ringing the bell at a mountain pass altar
in Himachal Pradesh, India.

Appendix II:
The True Faces of Reality

Reality can be described in many ways. I shall present three versions, or rather three levels of insight meant to describe the universe.

The top level, which we are all acquainted with, is the impression of the surroundings delivered by our senses. They offer sufficient information to yield a description of the world, but at the same time our eyes and ears have obvious limitations. You can see an insect, but you require a microscope to see bacteria. You can see the stars of the Milky Way, but far away galaxies require a telescope to see them. Humans live in a world delineated by the capacity of bodily organs; not only do we feel at home there, but until recently we were oblivious to anything else.

On the next level, reality has a lot more to offer. Even the ancient Greeks realized that the eyes do not catch everything in that it is impossible to see the unit of matter and referred to such units as atoms. We now know that what we call atoms can be split up into elementary particles, but the basic assumption that matter is an assembly of tiny units still stands.[6] By understanding the physics of elementary particles, and thus the actual structure of the cosmos, you have reached the second level of insight into reality. You have moved far from the realms of your perceptive organs, but not away from the sort of logic your brain has evolved for the purpose of understanding things.

In order to appreciate that there is an even deeper, third level of comprehension, you need to take a leap of faith away from the intuitive. We are adapted to live at the "surface," but can reach the second level by means of scientific instruments and logical deductions. The third, innermost face of reality requires a step into terrain unfamiliar to the human brain. If you are able to take this step, you will not only find a deeper understanding of the world, but also a platform for sensing God. Science admittedly appears somewhat blind-

---

[6] For an update on these units, see C. Quigg, "The Coming Revolutions in Particle Physics," *Scientific American* (February 2008): 38–45.

folded when moving into this deepest level, but that does not stop scientists from trying.[7]

The idea is that you need to go beyond a mere description of elementary particles in order to grasp the actual principles behind our Universe. The principles I am referring to are the forces that define the properties of the particles and describe how their interactions create a reality. Efforts to describe this deeper level are based primarily on the models referred to as relativity theory, quantum physics, and string theory. You need not despair if these theories seem far beyond your capacity to comprehend; the Nobel Prize winner in physics, Richard Feynman, claimed that no one understands quantum physics. In fact, we are not at all sure that our efforts are on the right track. Still, I shall offer my attempt at grasping what reality is really about.

––––––––

To start off, you need to have an idea as to what the three terms *quantum, field,* and *energy* mean.

Energy, time, and space can all be divided into related units referred to as "quanta." Max Planck was the first to suggest this, and the mathematical model on which these units are based thus bears his name: Planck's constant. It is best known as the theory of quantum mechanics. This constant allows us to calculate the actual size of the quanta; for example, the unit of length is ~1.6×10^{-35} m, and that of time, ~5.4×10^{-44} s. The elementary particles are still the smallest units of matter; it is their attributes that are based on quanta, including their mass. Einstein's famous formula, $E=mc^2$, describes how mass and energy are related to each other.

Most people are familiar with the concept of "field" in connection with gravitational or electromagnetic fields. A reasonable interpretation of the term is to say that it reflects forces with the capacity to impact on the quanta.

You are probably also familiar with *energy*. This phenomenon appears in many forms, such as the heat from a fire, muscle movement, the power of nuclear reactions, or mass; but these are all just manifestations of the same energy quanta. The different terms used

––––––––

[7] Several well-known scientists have made attempts at describing the true face of reality. See S. Hawking and L. Mlodinow, *A Briefer History of Time* (2008); or M. Bhaumik, *Code Named God* (2005). The latter offers God a comfortable seat in his description.

simply reflect how energy can reveal itself to our senses. The Universe contains a given amount of energy (or mass, since these two are convertible), but it can turn up at different places and in different forms.

A kindergarten offers a reasonable analogy to reality. That is, reality is simply the "playful behavior" of the enormous aggregation of quanta, or "kids," that comprise the Universe. They need, however, a playpen. This may have been present even before the Big Bang, as an entity referred to as the quantum vacuum. Once the quanta arrived on the scene, as a consequence of the Big Bang, four different fields were there to act as "nursery assistants" defining the rules of play.

Some scientists assume that originally there was only one field, the primary field, and that this field was present even before the quanta arrived. Moreover, within the miniature scale in which the quanta exist this is still the only field operating. What we are fairly sure of is that, since the playpen was filled with matter, four nursery assistants were there to share the job; at least this is the way it appears on the scale that we can examine with our present scientific tools. These four fields reflect the four basic forces of the Universe: gravitation, electromagnetism, the strong nuclear force, and the weak nuclear force. It is a paradox that we are equipped to relate to only one of them, gravitation, which is by far the weakest of the four.

To sum up, the Universe can be seen as a playpen in which one or as many as four fields rule the play of space, time, and energy quanta.

The energy quanta, including their manifestation as mass, are the more lively players; it is the macroscopic reflection of their actions our senses and brain are equipped to understand. If, however, you were the size of Planck's unit of space (i.e., some 10^{-35} m tall), and had the proper sensory equipment, reality would be a totally different experience. You would probably sense that the world was controlled by a single field. You might indeed add some special significance to this field—for example, referring to it as God.

The important point is that reality at the fundamental level reflects a sort of plan. For the Universe to happen, "something" somehow had to set the theater in motion and take the role of director as the performance unfolds. The rest is history—some 13.7 billion years of it. The pantheist may view the primary field as God—possibly throwing in the quanta as well. The panentheists like to offer God the credit for kick-starting the process, with the further capacity of intervention for those who believe in an intervening God. Moreover, with the exception of Divine intervention, the above semantic options with regard to defining God are perfectly aligned with science. In fact, as I see it, at the deepest level the model of reality begs for the introduction of the concept of Divinity.

A Portuguese cat watching over a local version of the annunciation.

Appendix III:
Religion: The Role of the Genes

Is the capacity to sense the Divine ingrained in our genes? Does our religious engagement reflect human nature? I shall explain why I believe both answers to be "yes."[8]

Perhaps the most important observation supporting this answer is that more or less every culture includes conceptions of a religious nature. When a type of behavior is present around the globe, it most likely reflects an innate disposition. That is to say, the genes push us toward engaging in God, as they push us to fall in love or eat when hungry. It is also striking that the various religious myths have so much in common—even when collected from indigenous people on the opposite sides of the globe.

Another relevant observation is the central role of religion in society. As a biologist I expect there to be a correspondence between the amount of time and resources that are used for a particular purpose and to what extent that purpose represents an innate inclination. Whether in tribal society or industrialized nations, devotion occupies a significant proportion of a person's daily or weekly routine. It is also tempting to point out that we are talking about an entity with considerable power of influence. The feelings associated with worship dominate both mind and behavior in a significant proportion of the population. In fact, there appear to be neural circuits designed for the purpose of focusing our attention on God, and we have some clues as to which parts of the brain are involved. Moreover, the tendency toward religious engagement has an inherent component, and at least one specific gene (VMAT2) has been suggested to be involved.[9]

---

[8] For a more comprehensive discussion, see D. S. Wilson, *Darwin's Cathedral—Evolution, Religion and the Nature of Society* (2002); or B. Grinde, "The Biology of Religion: A Darwinian Gospel," *Journal of Social and Evolutionary Systems* 21 (1998): 19–28.

[9] A. B. Newberg, E. G. d'Aquili, and V. Rause, *Why God Won't Go Away* (2001); M. Beauregard and D. O'Leary, *The Spiritual Brain: A Neuroscientist's Case for the Existence of the Soul* (2007). As to the genetics, see D. Hamer, *The God Gene* (2004).

In combination, these observations offer considerable evidence for the proposition that we are born with a religious disposition. That is not to say that one gene or for that matter several genes are dedicated to the task of making us true believers. The property is rather a consequence of minor mutations in a large number of genes whose task it is to construct the brain. Together these changes created a brain with slightly altered properties—a brain inclined to sense a Divine power.

Some scientists consider religion to be a byproduct of other properties laid down by evolution; for example, our propensity for submission to authority, the capacity to wonder about reality, and our need for security once the intellect laid bare the uncertainty of existence.[10] The claim that evolution inclined us toward a religious disposition is reasonably compatible with this stance. It is still a question of genetic mutations moving our thoughts in the direction of accepting Divinity. In my mind, the main issue is to what extent religion itself was instrumental in inducing these changes; that is, did a religious propensity offer any evolutionary advantages to early man? Alternatively, was it simply a question of selection for other characteristics that happened, as a byproduct, to make us religious? In short, did religion help us survive?

The literature I have referred to suggests a long list of possible evolutionary advantages, perhaps the most important being that religion made the tribe a more cohesive unit. A system of belief made it easier to devise, and make people accept, rules of conduct, which again made the tribe stronger.

Even as faith is based on an innate tendency, faith does not imply that everybody will necessarily be religious. We are also equipped with innate tendencies toward falling in love or enjoying music, but not everyone engages in these options either. Dispositions are there to influence us but cannot, as a general rule, enforce a certain type of behavior. Moreover, there are significant variations as to how strongly different individuals feel or react to dispositions. Consider the basic urge to eat when your brain engages its hunger module; people with anorexia either do not recognize the signals or refuse to heed them.

----

[10] See, for example, S. Atran, *In God We Trust: The Evolutionary Landscape of Religion* (2002).

A common objection to the existence of anything Divine is that God is simply a concept floating around in our minds.

Life revolves around experiences; that is, it revolves around certain forms of brain activity. Some experiences are associated with objects, or conditions, that have a correlate outside our heads, while others reflect solely internal affairs. People claim, for example, that "love is in the air," while biologically speaking it is just a feeling resting inside our brains. Then again, love normally involves someone in addition to yourself.

God too has a correlate in the form of brain activity, as do our notions of elementary particles. Neither God, nor the particles, can be seen. Yet the scientists will certainly claim that the particles have an existence outside the brain; people of faith will take a similar stance with regard to the Divine. As discussed in Appendix II: *The True Faces of Reality,* p. 191, if God represents the forces and entities defining the Universe at the most profound level, then God certainly has a tangible foothold in the real world. This stance makes sense to me, but in the end it is a choice of philosophy, or of semantics if you prefer. The portraits we paint of God will necessarily reflect the corresponding brain activity, as will the models we make for elementary particles.

This book assumes God to be a permeating quality of the Universe, as well as a force behind its very existence. A consequence of that stance is that God in some way is responsible for the process of evolution. Thus, even if we are able to explain why the concept of God exists in genetic, neurological, and evolutionary terms, it is still formally correct to consider humans to be God's creation. This realization suggests a more profound reason for why we evolved the capacity to sense the presence of a Divine Force.

The sun, or maybe God, shines on the western coast of Norway.

Appendix IV:
Is There Anybody Out There?

The sun has eight planets as well as four "dwarf planets" (known as plutoids, and which include Pluto), but only one planet is (today) suitable for life. The particular and fine-tuned attributes of Earth appear to be not only ideal for the evolution of life forms, but also highly unique.

If life exists elsewhere in the Universe, it is most likely based on pretty much the same chemistry; that is to say, it is founded on the peculiar features of carbon. In that case, in order to harbor life, other planets need to resemble our planet—certainly if life is to evolve toward intelligent forms. Might Earth be one of a kind?

It is difficult to study planets outside our solar system because they reveal few clues as to their existence. Still, astronomers have discovered hundreds of planets circling stars in our part of the Milky Way. Most of these are giant gas planets, somewhat like Jupiter and Saturn, and thus totally useless as habitat. However, the present technology for finding planets selects for this type, and presumably there are a lot of undiscovered smaller planets circling the same stars. Although the Earth is so exceptional that finding anything like it nearby is unlikely, we are closing in on planets with some resemblance.[11]

The Milky Way includes roughly 300 billion stars. The observable part of the Universe has some 100 billion galaxies, and the total number of stars has been estimated to be 7×10^{22}. Even with only one planet on the average for each star, there should be a reasonable number of choices, something to suit anyone's taste.

Life based on carbon has a rather exclusive taste, but as the basic physical rules are the same all over the Universe, it would seem statistically highly likely that the required conditions have been repeated several times. And as life also is a consequence of the same laws of physics, one might expect the process of evolution to per-

---

[11] See G. Marcy, "Water World Larger Than Earth," *Nature* 462 (2009): 853–54.

form similar miracles elsewhere. Unless, of course, some Divine entity interfered and made Earth the chosen one.

A solar system like ours would not appear until the Universe had become at least a few billion years old. The evolution of intelligent life required another four billion to five billion years. The Universe, however, has been around for more than 13 billion years, which implies that at least for the last five billion years intelligent life forms may exist somewhere out there—in a galaxy far from ours. And, if they proved to be sufficiently intelligent not to destroy the life-giving qualities of their planet, they may still hang around, pondering about God and the meaning of life.

Anyone is free to make a guess as to whether we are alone or not, because science has not yet provided any answer. Whoever is out there, we shall never meet them. To "hear" from them in the form of radio signals is a slightly less desperate idea, but, unfortunately, extremely unlikely.

The problem is distances. Planets suitable for sustaining life that could communicate with us are probably rare. Our closest galactic neighbor, Andromeda, is 2.5 million light years away. Thus, even the fastest of signals (based on electromagnetic radiation, which includes radio waves) requires 2.5 million years to reach us. The Milky Way is stretched out over 100,000 light years, and even the closest stars, the Alpha Centauri group, are more than four light years away. With extreme luck, there could be intelligent life on stars in our corner of the galaxy, and with even more luck they would be sufficiently sociable to send out signals in an attempt to set up an interstar communication system. Not knowing about us, they would need to broadcast in every direction, with transmitters of enormous power. Moreover, if you feel that the internet can be slow, consider waiting several, possibly millions of years for a simple answer.

Then again, some people never give up. There are those who try to tune in to possible attempts at communicating, primarily focusing on the nearer stars. They have tried for 50 years but so far have not received a single beep. That, however, does not discourage a true seeker of extraterrestrial life; with the help of a new, more powerful antenna, they expect that over the next 20 years they should be able to examine a million stars in their search of meaningful broadcasts.[12]

The number of stars and planets does improve the odds, but overall it seems highly unlikely that we shall find companionship within a distance that allows for communication. With all due respect, astrobiology is likely to remain what it is today—the only science without any object to investigate.[13]

How about life based on a different chemistry? In that case the planetary requirements would also be different—and perhaps less exclusive. Silicon seems to be the one that is a vaguely realistic alternative to carbon.[14]

Silicon is indeed the element most closely resembling carbon, and it is actually a major component of most earth rocks. Furthermore, it happens to be a key element in the production of chips for computers. Thus, on this planet the closest you would get to a silicon-organism would be your laptop; but possibly on some planet in a murky corner of a shaky galaxy your computer might have distant cousins walking around and setting up carbon-based computers.

It is, however, more likely that we, rather than our computers, have relatives out there. Life based on our chemistry seems more realistic due to the following four observations:

1. Life on Earth depends on elements that are particularly prevalent in the Universe.

2. We are based on carbon even though silicon happens to be a more common element on Earth.

3. Upon considering all the elements, not one seems as suitable to form a variety of complex molecules as carbon. Silicon readily

---

[12] The more serious attempts are performed by the SETI Institute (Search for Extra-Terrestrial Intelligence). See Z. Merali, "Is There Anybody Out There?" *New Scientist* (February 9, 2008): 8–9.

[13] For those who still retain an interest, see I. Gilmour and M. A. Sephton, *An Introduction to Astrobiology* (2004).

[14] D. Fox, "Life, But Not As We Know It," *New Scientist* (June 9, 2007): 35–39.

bonds to other atoms, such as oxygen, but the bonding tends to be too stable. Silicon compounds are perfect for building rocks, but life depends on a constant remake of molecules.

4. Carbon-based molecules appear to be common outside the Earth, since we find them on meteorites. Silicon is also common as a constituent of rocks, but while extraterrestrial silicon compounds are simple and boring, there is more of a variety of carbon molecules.

———

Carbon is number four on the prevalence list of elements in the Universe, and silicon number eight. It is a fascinating fact that these two elements are produced in such quantities, and that they are both amply present on Earth. Carbon may be here to produce us, while silicon is here to help us. Besides doing what it takes for our computers, silicon has an attribute that can help save the planet: The element allows us to harness the energy of the photons emitted by the sun and convert it to electrical current. This is what takes place in a solar cell. As sunshine is likely to be around five billion years longer than oil, silicon may fuel the gadgets of the future population into eternity.

———

There are two important, practical conclusions to be drawn from the above text: One, if we destroy this planet, there is nowhere else to go; and two, there is nobody out there to help us—with the possible exception of God.

Appendix V:
Be Conscious of Your Subconscious

All mammals have some form of consciousness. The main difference is to what extent they have self-awareness; that is, whether they consider themselves as separate entities and can reflect on the difference between you and me. Humans are the experts. We have brought both self-awareness and thus insight, which are related to the question of who we are, to a much higher level than any other animals. Yet, we are not the only species having a clue as to what or who we are. The mirror test was invented to examine this capacity. You mark a dot on the forehead of the animal and place the animal in front of a mirror. A dog might attack the mirror, which means it flunks the test for self-awareness. A chimpanzee or bonobo, on the other hand, will probably start to probe the mark on the forehead with a finger, knowing the animal in the mirror is itself. Apparently

The ghost of a monk outside a remote church
on the island of Naxos, Greece.

203

not just apes, but also elephants, dolphins, and whales have some sort of self-awareness.

Self-awareness, particularly in the extreme human form, is a rather daring experiment of evolution. One consequence is an ego with the idea that it is the boss of its own life. In other words, the ego assumes it can control the body harboring it, while in a biological sense, the genes are the obvious owners of the body. The problem is that the ego may initiate silly ideas of considerable detriment to the genes, such as committing suicide.

Evolution is not completely stupid. Consequently it has introduced distinct limitations as to what one's self-aware ego is allowed to engage in. Most of the processes going on in the brain are hidden from consciousness. In fact, the subconscious parts of the brain not only control a long list of bodily processes, such as the heart beat and the formation of urine, but they also send signals that may have a considerable impact on decisions made by the conscious brain. The subconscious pushes our thoughts and behavior in various directions without us being aware of what is going on. For example, if one spots an object on the ground that remotely resembles a snake, one may react with fear before having time to evaluate whether the object really poses any danger.

The subconscious has something to say even when engaged in what may be considered personal commitments, such as creativity, learning, or talking. If you try to recall a name, you will typically need to wait for the subconscious to go through the archives of memory to find it for you. When children learn to speak, they engage innate mechanisms of language acquisition controlled by the subconscious. If you require inspiration in connection with the novel you are writing, you often wait for the subconscious to pop out ideas. The conscious part of the brain may get all the credit, but it is actually a somewhat clumsy entity with limited capacity for doing anything. What it has is an unlimited propensity for stealing the attention from your better part: the subconscious you.

In short, consciousness is only one of a long list of features harbored in the brain, a feature that your subconscious brain turns on or off according to whether it is needed or not. In fact, we know something about the "switch" used. The brain can be divided into two main parts: the cortex and the brain stem. Presumably consciousness uses primarily parts of the cortex, while the subconscious owns most of the remaining brain structures. The switch is apparently located in a lump of nerve tissue, referred to as the thalamus, which lies at the top of the brain stem and just beneath the cortex. In one particular case, a patient had been in a coma for six years when the doctors managed to turn on part of his conscious functions again. They did so by sending electrical stimuli to a particular area within his thalamus.[15]

Your subconscious functions are never relieved of duty. At night they are there alone; if, however, something important should happen, something requiring your awareness, they wake you up. It could be your baby crying, or a sound vaguely suggesting an animal of prey, or in these days perhaps a burglar. The conscious evolved because it is better equipped to tackle interactions with the more unpredictable features of the environment; when called for, the genes of course make sure you take on this responsibility. Thus, every morning, the subconscious decides that you have had enough time off, and that your services are required. The switch is turned to on—and yes, your self-awareness is suddenly back on the job your genes set it up for.

As already mentioned, consciousness is a somewhat awkward entity with direct access to only a small part of your brain. Consider tasks where you require fine-tuned muscle movements, such as playing tennis or golf. You need to relinquish control over your arms and let the subconscious do the job. You simply tell the subconscious what should happen to the ball, and then let the "instincts" manage the muscles. Any complex, coordinated movement requires practice, but once a reasonable template for exerting the move has been established, the more common mistake is to *not* release control; that is, you do not trust your subconscious to do the job better.

Running is easier. You decide the direction, your eyes feed the brain with relevant information about the terrain, and based on this your subconscious supervises muscle movements. For most people it is obvious that the legs need to be controlled by the subconscious autopilot. The difference between running and playing tennis is that the former is an activity evolution has shaped us for, while the latter is an odd game invented to test your aptitude.

---

[15] M. N. Shadlen and R. Kiani, "An Awakening," *Nature* 448 (2007): 539–40.

The subconscious is not just one particular state of mind. A person in a coma is in a very different situation compared to a patient under anesthesia. Sleep includes two rather different stages: One is calm and "low key"; the other is characterized by rapid eye movements (REM-sleep) and concomitant brain activity that typically involves dreaming.

Neither is there a single state of being conscious. It is a question of several related conditions that are perceived differently. If you are half asleep, or totally exhausted, the way you experience reality is different when compared to focusing on a lecture. Psychoactive substances, which is to say anything from alcohol to LSD, also change the way you experience life, and so also may diseases such as schizophrenia or epilepsy.

There is also a particular state of mind associated with the experience of being in touch with the Divine. Those with the talent to enter this condition describe it in very positive terms—perhaps it is the best type of conscious experience available.

Appendix VI:
Meditation

The concept of meditation covers a range of techniques whose purpose is to have an impact on your brain in a positive way,. A central element is to enable you to disconnect from your surroundings and focus on your internal mind. The focus may be directed at sensual experiences—for example, breathing, or the passage of air through the nose—or in some cases it may be directed inward at feelings such as compassion, or just "inward" at nothing in particular. In the more common forms of meditation, the objective may be described as retaining consciousness (i.e., not to fall asleep), but relieving the conscious of any task.

Meditators in Auroville, India, a city where meditation
is considered a means to reform the Earth.

I shall try to explain what I believe meditation is all about, the purpose being to help the uninitiated reader develop a capacity for personal meditative experiences.[16]

Meditative techniques induce internal sensations by activating certain parts of the brain. At present we do know something about which parts of the brain are involved. The act is typically described as an enjoyable experience, but more important, the effort can cause lasting changes in the brain when performed regularly. Such changes have indeed been documented, for example, in terms of an improved capacity to retain focus on a task.

Another way of describing meditation is to consider it as a means to reach a particular state of mind. This state can be depicted as "effortless attentiveness." Both body and brain are relaxed, and you feel a euphoric well-being; you are present somewhere deep inside yourself, while the physical surroundings seem far away. Some people describe the experience as a "oneness with all," and may give it religious significance. There is actually a connection between meditation and religion in that most creeds include some form of meditative practices; moreover, the techniques were probably first devised in connection with religious activity. So, is this state of mind really being in touch with the Divine?

The answer is primarily a question of whether or not you prefer to see things in a religious context. There are similarities between the experience of being in touch with God as induced, for example, by prayer, and the experience even atheists can have during meditation; however, whether you consider it religious or not, meditation can have a positive effect on health and quality of life.[17]

The secular purpose of meditation is primarily to relieve stress. You reduce stress by teaching the conscious brain to calm down and not be bothered by all the quandaries associated with living. Yet,

---

[16] The report, *Meditation Practices for Health: State of the Research* (2007), offers a comprehensive and objective update. It was commissioned by the U. S. Government, and is available at:
http://www.ahrq.gov/downloads/pub/evidence/pdf/meditation/medit.pdf
[17] Richard Davidson has done a lot of serious research on meditation. For a scientific presentation see, for example, A. Lutz, H. A. Slagter, J. D. Dunne, and R. J. Davidson "Attention Regulation and Monitoring in Meditation," *Trends in Cognitive Sciences* 12 (2008): 163–69.

meditation is not simply a form of rest as an alternative to sleep; it is a bit more demanding. Typically you sit down in a quiet place with your eyes closed. Usually, a lotus position is fine for those who are trained to sit like that; otherwise a chair is better. The back should preferably be erect. If you sink down, the mind is easily directed toward sleep; on the other hand, if you stand or walk, some of your attention is required elsewhere. It is possible to enter a meditative state regardless of place or position, but it is easier, particularly for a novice, to follow the above suggestions.

So far the task is simple. The challenge is to get rid of all the thoughts that constantly pop up in your mind and catch your attention. The meditative state requires that you rid the mind of those kinds of matters. Consciousness, however, is not designed for idleness: To stop thinking is thus a lot more difficult than simply to shut your eyes. The meditative techniques are typically aimed at helping you in this endeavor. Relaxation in general depends on getting rid of worries and other stressful thoughts. Once you learn to disengage by entering a meditative state, it is also easier to keep your mind relaxed in daily life.

Some schools of meditation supply you with a *mantra*. A mantra is a simple combination of sounds, preferably without any meaning, which you keep repeating either inside yourself or as a form of chanting. The sounds may be "a-uhm" or "a-ing," while others prefer to use whole sentences with a content that may impact on your mentality, such as "I feel fine." In religious forms of meditation, practitioners may prefer to repeat simple prayers. The main point of the mantra is to offer the mind something to hang on to, something that requires a minimal effort. In that way it is easier to avoid having the mind getting caught up in strings of thoughts; consequently you are more likely to calm down. As an alternative to a mantra, you may focus on your breathing—sensing the in-and-out movement of air. The experienced meditator may not need these tools, but for the novice it is difficult to enter a state where thoughts and distractions do not catch your attention.

When nothing occupies your mind, you may sense a deep relaxation. It is a pleasant condition where the mind seems to be "floating." Getting there is the object of meditation.

Even with advanced meditators, outside sounds or internal ideas easily catch one's attention. The point is to let them go at an early stage and thus get back to the internal focus. One advice is to consider the distractions as twigs floating by on a stream. Let them pass without causing any fuss. If you pick them up, they take control of you, and even using a conscious effort to keep them away is like building a dam that just retains them.

In addition to the above suggestions, there are certain means that can be used to boost the meditative effort. Prior to meditation you may practice yoga or listen to calming music. The idea is that the relaxing qualities of these activities will help set both body and mind in the right mood for meditation. Autogenic training is a related technique. It is a form of self-hypnosis; you sit or lie down while telling yourself that the arm is warm and heavy and that there is no muscle tonus left. By consecutively focusing on each part of the body in this way, you end up with all muscles in a relaxed state; and by letting your body unwind like that, you calm down your mind as well.

Meditation may be used for more than just relaxation: It can be a way to exercise the brain. Any part of the brain, or body, will tend to expand, or improve, if used repeatedly. Muscles become stronger, and brain modules get more dominant in their impact on consciousness. There *are* parts of the brain, however, that you may *not* want to practice; for example, the structures involved in anxiety. But other elements are definitely worth some work: For instance, in the tradition of Tibetan Buddhism people meditate on compassion as a way to develop kindness, which is not a bad idea, but you can also focus your meditative effort on modules involved in happiness or in the bliss, or peak experience, related to experiencing God. If you manage to activate relevant centers, not only does it boost your immediate joy while meditating, but by strengthening these functions, they are also more easily activated while not in a meditative state. The art is to find out how.

The top runners of the world most likely run faster than any Stone Age person was ever able to, and elite chess players are more focused. It is all about training certain components of mind and body in an optimal way. Today we know a lot more about how to optimize the effort; thus, the best keep getting better. It is possible to develop the capacity to calm the brain and set the modules of happiness in focus. Meditation offers a relevant approach. Consequently, present-day humans are in a position to obtain a quality of life superior to anything experienced before in the history of life on Planet Earth.

Three islands pointing to the setting sun, off the western coast of Sweden.

INDEX

A

Abraham, 56
adrenalin, 129, 130
Africa, 106, 107, 110, 11, 114, 134,
    182
Age of Enlightenment, 5, 187
aggression, vii, 50, 141, 142, 156, 176
aggressive behavior, 155
aging, 104, 105, 140
agnosticism, 188
agriculture, 114, 154, 181
Ainsworth, C., 102
Akbar, 57, 58
Albania, 172
Allen, J. F., 96
Alpha Centauri group, 200
altruism, 19, 147
Andromeda Galaxy), 179, 200
anesthesia, 206
anorexia, 196
Antarctic krill, 112
anthropic cosmological principle, 27
anthropomorphize, 49
anxiety, 126, 133, 136, 137, 139
    and brain, 126
ape(s), 105, 106, 147, 148, 156
aphids, 104
Archaea, 91
Aristotle, 56
arthropod(s), 100–1
Asoka, 57
asteroid(s), 79, 80, 102
astrobiology, 201
atheist(s), 9, 12, 13, 16, 18. 24, 34, 39,
    43, 66, 159, 163, 167, 172, 187,
    208
    and Einstein, 25
atmosphere, 80, 95–96
    of Earth, 79
    and plants, 178
atoms, 23, 28, 32, 59, 60, 69, 70. 74,
    78, 79, 80, 81, 85, 86, 88, 94,
    171, 174, 179, 191, 202
    hydrogen, 25, 72
atomic bomb, 77
Atran, S., 196

Auroville, 10, 162, 207
autogenic training, 210
autopilot, 205

B

baboons, 136
bacteria, bacterial, 88, 90, 91, 96, 97,
    98, 102, 104, 143, 153, 174, 180,
    181, 191
    cells, 143
    infection, 136
Baha'u'llah, 56, 57, 58
Balter, M., 127
Barcelo, C., 48
Barger, A. J., 74
Barrett, L., 106
Barrow, J. D., 27
Battersby, S., 82, 179
Beauregard, M., 59, 160
Begun, D. R., 106
Behe, M. J., 188
Bhaumik, M., 192
Bible, ix, 5, 14, 17, 39, 43, 63, 65, 66,
    68, 77, 84, 147, 172, 187, 188
Big Bang, 23, 24, 25, 30, 48, 67, 68,
    73, 82, 180, 193
biomass, 112
biotechnology, 115, 176
birds, 101, 142, 145
Biswas-Diener, R., 122
black hole, 48, 76, 170, 171
Blanke, O., 59
bonobo(s), 106, 154, 156, 203
Boyer, P., 52
Brahman, 52
brain(s), 3, 46, 47, 49, 50, 59, 84, 99,
    100, 105, 108, 109, 124, 127,
    128, 130, 131, 133, 134, 137,
    140, 143, 146, 147, 149, 150,
    153, 156, 160, 162, 167, 168,
    191, 195, 196, 197, 204, 205,
    206, 207, 208, 210
    and behavior, 126
    design of, 126
    evolution of, 49, 126, 191
    and behavior, 126

213

About the Author

Bjørn Grinde (born 1952) received his education in natural sciences, psychology, and anthropology from the University of Oslo, with a Dr. Scient. (1981) and a Dr. Philos. (1984) in biology. He is presently employed as Chief Scientist at the Division of Mental Health, Norwegian Institute of Public Health, and as a professor at the University of Oslo. His scientific production (some 120 papers) is related to genetics, microbiology, molecular biology, and human behavior. A lasting focus has been to understand the process of evolution. He has previously served as a professor at the Medical Faculty, University of Bergen, and worked as a scientist in the United States and Japan.

Human behavior has been a particular interest for almost four decades. He believes that knowledge about how evolution has shaped the human mind may help us improve conditions for mankind. This conviction has led to the publication of two popular books, one in Norwegian, *Genene–Din Indre Guru* (Grøndahl Dreyer, 1996), and one published in the United States, *Darwinian Happiness–Evolution as a Guide for Living and Understanding Human Behavior* (Darwin Press, 2002). The present book is based on the author's translation from his original work in Norwegian, *GUD–en vitenskapelig oppdatering* (2008).

Grinde is a member of the Human Behavior and Evolution Society and the International Society for Human Ethology. Besides research, he has been actively engaged in popularizing science—by writing articles regularly for newspapers and magazines and by participating in radio and TV programs for the Norwegian Broadcasting System. He enjoys nature, both in the human form, and in the absence of humans, with a particular fondness for mountains. He is not associated with any religious denomination.